GEORGE ADAMSKI

A HERALD FOR
THE SPACE BROTHERS

GEORGE ADAMSKI

A HERALD FOR
THE SPACE BROTHERS

GERARD AARTSEN

George Adamski – A Herald for the Space Brothers
First published August 2010
Second edition: January 2012

Copyright © 2010 Gerard Aartsen, Amsterdam, the Netherlands.

Portions of this book © G.A.F. International/George Adamski Foundation, Vista, Cal., USA (www.adamskifoundation.com). Permission granted by copyright holders, 2010. Permission for use of copyrighted G.A.F. International materials does not imply that the Foundation necessarily agrees with the views expressed in this work.

Photo credits: p.vi: Courtesy Timothy Good; pp.10 and 44: Copyright © G.A.F. International/George Adamski Foundation, Vista, Calif.; pp.21 and 73: Used with permission from the Leslie Estate, Ireland; p.75: UCLA Charles E. Young Research Library Department of Special Collections, Los Angeles Daily News Photographic Archives. Copyright © Regents of the University of California, UCLA Library.

All rights reserved. No part of this book may be reproduced by any means and in any form whatsoever without written permission from the copyright holder(s), except for brief quotations in reviews.

ISBN-13/EAN-13: 978-90-815495-2-3

Published by BGA Publications, Amsterdam, the Netherlands.
www.bgapublications.nl

Printed and distributed by LightningSource.

Typeset in Calisto MT.

Cover design: Jan Henkes.

Cover photograph: Space ship over the airport of the city of Hangzhou, China, taken 7 July 2010. Photographer unknown.

To Benjamin Creme,
himself a herald, and
an inspiring and humbling example
of service to humanity.

George Adamski (1891-1965)

Contents

Preface ix

Part One: The Man and His Mission 1

1. The Backdrop:
   Foregone conclusions, or wisdom foregone? 3
2. The Man:
   'Who *are* you, George?' 19
3. The Mission:
   For the betterment of all 37
4. The Teaching:
   Universal brotherhood, individual responsibility 69

Part Two: Writings 99

The Magnificent Perception (1961) 101

The Space People (1964) 111

Epilogue 127

Appendix

George Adamski publications 131

Other sources 137

Index 139

List of illustrations

1. George Adamski vi
2. Venusian scout ship 10
3. Adamski and Leslie at Palomar 21
4. US ad for *The Scoriton Mystery* (1968) 30
5. Mothership photographed by a Space Brother 44
6. Early announcement Get Acquainted Program 58
7. Contact list Get Acquainted Program 62
8. Adamski at Palomar Gardens, circa 1954 73
9. Adamski at Laguna Beach, 1938 75
10. First page of manuscript for 'The Space People' 110

Preface

Steeped as they were in the materialistic world view so dominant in the 20th century, it didn't take most members of the scientific community and the media much time to doubt, denounce and discard the facts and experiences which George Adamski described in the books that propelled him into the international limelight in the 1950s, *Flying Saucers Have Landed* and *Inside the Space Ships*.

In addition, governments and the military had everything to lose from a general awareness that humanity is not alone in the Universe, or even in our own solar system. Yet, educating the public about the reality of Life on and from other planets was precisely the mission which Adamski had taken upon himself, and even in death he continues to be slandered for his pains.

Once our space probes had established that life as we know it was not possible on the dense-physical levels of planets like Mars and Venus, Adamski's claims of having photographed space ships and meeting people from these planets were ridiculed, while skeptics tried to belittle him by cooking up lies about his profession, his character and his intentions, and covert government operations were allowed to go all-out to confuse the public mind about the true nature of the UFO phenomenon.

Over the years much has been said and written about the man who is generally considered the first of the 'contactees' – very little of which involved much open-mindedness and most of it being malicious theories, accusations, derogatory comments, half-truths and outright lies. Only a handful of authors, if that many, thought Adamski worthy of serious investigation.

While most authors, sympathetic or skeptic, busied themselves proving or disproving, as the case may be, Adamski's claims about his experiences with UFOs and their occupants, he himself persevered and worked as hard as ever to help a deeply divided world obtain a sense of the fundamental oneness underlying all expressions of the universal life, which he experienced and was taught by his extraterrestrial contacts. What he lacked, perhaps, in sophistication he made up for in urgency and steadfastness of purpose.

Rather than a proper biography which traces the life

PREFACE

of its subject, this book is more of a monograph about the scope and significance of Adamski's work, which is reappraised here in light of the spiritual realities of life with the emergence into full public view of our Elder Brothers – the Masters of Wisdom of the Spiritual Hierarchy, headed by the World Teacher – and the Space Brothers from our neighbouring planets, at the dawn of the new cosmic cycle of Aquarius.[1]

As these realities become clearer to more people every day, it will be seen that Adamski was hardly the "crackpot from California" that *Time* magazine and others made him out to be[2], but a visionary teacher who was far ahead of the small minds that were waging a cold war against not just political opponents, but against the *fact* of our interplanetary brotherhood, of which George Adamski was the bravest messenger.

Gerard Aartsen
Amsterdam, May 2010

Acknowledgements
The author wishes to express his gratitude to Glenn Steckling of the George Adamski Foundation in Vista, California, USA, for their kind permission to use some of George Adamski's photographs and to reprint samples of his writings. He is also indebted to Tamae Ishiwatari of Tokyo, Japan; Anders Liljegren at the Archives For UFO Research (AFU) in Norrkoping, Sweden; author Timothy Good of Beckenham, England; Sammy Leslie of the Castle Leslie Estate in Glaslough, Ireland; and Miguel

Rubio of Amsterdam, the Netherlands, for their invaluable help with other materials. Special thanks go to Jan Henkes, of Zutphen, the Netherlands, for designing the cover. Finally, the author is heavily indebted to Benjamin Creme of London, England, for his indefatigable elucidation of the Ageless Wisdom teachings.

Notes

1 Far from being a 1960s hippie invention, this is an astronomical fact that can be verified by visiting any observatory. "It is the result of the movement of our solar system around the heavens in relation to the constellations of the zodiac... Approximately every 2,150 years (...) our sun comes into an alignment, an energetic relationship, with each of the constellations." (Benjamin Creme (2001), *The Great Approach*, p.4) According to the Ageless Wisdom teaching, at the dawn or close of every age a World Teacher is sent into the world to reveal to humanity a new aspect of the plan of evolution.
2 'The Queen & The Saucers', *Time* magazine, 1 June 1959 (www.time.com/time/magazine/article/0,9171,811123,00.html).

PART ONE:
THE MAN AND HIS MISSION

1. The Backdrop:

"Of all the contactees, Adamski attracted the most controversy and odium; and none but a man of his strength of character could have survived the onslaught..."
—Co-author Desmond Leslie, ***Flying Saucers Have Landed*** (Revised and Enlarged edition, 1970)

Foregone conclusions, or wisdom foregone?

The significance of the mission which George Adamski had taken upon himself can only be properly understood in the context of the political and scientific circumstances of his day. Perhaps especially so for younger readers who have grown up without the psychological threat of the decades-long stand-off between the USA and the former Soviet Union – the Cold War, as well as without the excitement of the early decades of space exploration. While looking at these, we will also be looking at the circumstances surrounding the controversies that arose around some of Adamski's claims, to re-frame the discussion about the relevance of his work.

Politics as usual

After having successfully co-operated to defeat the Nazi attempts of subjecting humanity to their utterly separative and grossly materialistic world view, the victorious allies quickly took up their ideological positions, endeavouring to dominate as large a part of the world as possible with their respective, and therefore limited, ideologies. The Americans and their allies professed to adhere to the concept of freedom (in the shape of 'democracy'), while the Russians claimed allegiance to justice (in the shape of 'communism'), both to the exclusion of the other universal concept.[1] But, as the current world situation shows in no uncertain terms, freedom for one is non-existent if it depends on the lack of it for another. Similarly, justice can only exist if it exists for all.

As a result, while the world was still reeling from the disastrous effects of the Second World War, it soon found itself on the brink of another war, this time of ideologies, with the added threat of both camps possessing, or in the process of obtaining, the most destructive invention of mankind to date – the atom bomb. Sadly, while World War II could be seen as the fundamental struggle for the victory of the divine nature of man[2], the conflict of the subsequent Cold War raged over two concepts which humanity will find to be inseparably linked if it is to realize its essential oneness and so express its divine nature – not as an ideal but in actuality.

Seen in the light of the fierce enmity that prevailed between the USA and Russia as the major powers in the

1950s, it will not have helped his cause when Adamski stated that the Space Brothers – about whose existence, visits and teachings it was his mission to educate the world – do not support any specific form of society on Earth, including the American variety. In fact, he said, "Such support would be complying with our custom of divisions. They recognize no false divisions of any kind. (…) They are non-political and non-sectarian, recognizing all mankind as brothers and sisters. Their interest lies in humanity as a whole wherever they find it; whether on our planet or elsewhere in the vast universe. But (…) they will support no one in hostility."[3]

When asked if the Space Brothers have what we would call a "Socialistic type of life", Adamski may have made matters worse when he replied: "I do not know what the word Socialism is supposed to represent. The word social means to be congenial and respect your fellow being. Jesus taught equality made up of many talents; the Space People live this Cosmic Law instead of the 'isms' that we proclaim."[4]

According to Adamski, the Space Brothers are so far ahead of us because "in divisions, we live as strangers to another. In brotherhood, they live in peace and harmony."[5]

The problem with science

The 1950s must have been an exciting time for space scientists, even without the sighting of UFOs which gained the attention of the mass media when US pilot Kenneth Arnold famously reported, on 24 June 1947, having seen nine unusual flying objects over the state of Washington. The world's two remaining superpowers had every intention of staying ahead of their competitor, and their space programmes only reflected their political and military ambitions.

When Adamski, as a confirmed non-academic[6], came along and published his detailed accounts of life on the very planets which state-of-the-art space probes were just showing to be incapable of supporting life as we know it on planet Earth, the scientific community as a whole was not impressed. Of course, they had no clue that what Adamski had seen with his own eyes defies the tyranny of physical-plane empiricism which has kept science in thrall since it haughtily brushed aside the propositions of the Ageless Wisdom teaching as given out by Helena P. Blavatsky and Alice A. Bailey, that there are higher levels of material reality than the three that science currently recognizes – the dense-physical, the liquid and the gaseous.

If the establishment hadn't locked up Wilhelm Reich and thrown away the key for him to die in prison, his discoveries would have opened vistas into these higher planes of matter – etheric matter as they are referred to by esotericists – which Reich had discovered and which he called orgone. It is on these higher planes of matter, as invisible as electricity or magnetism, but just as real, on which life on the other planets exists. In the process our scientists would have solved the riddle of the largest part of the physical universe – 'dark matter' – eluding our view, according to their own calculations, which they are now spending billions of dollars on proving with CERN's particle accelerator.[7] Speaking from his background as a student of the teachings given through H.P. Blavatsky and Alice A. Bailey, esotericist Benjamin Creme put it most aptly when he said: "We can build cyclotrons that are 23 kilometres long and take 20 years to build and cost billions of dollars. But if you ask an esotericist he will tell you the answers. For free. In a minute."[8]

Nevertheless, writes Adamski, "[s]ome scientists, I know, are receiving help from the space people; and many admit what they are 'getting' is beyond anything known or written in our present textbooks. Still, much information must be withheld. (...) We have much growing to do before it will be safe for us to be given a full understanding of the natural forces that they have harnessed for propelling their ships."[9]

Moreover, Adamski himself knew that, "...all Nature is etheric; whether in a form or formless state. The highest understandable manifestations are invisible gases out of which all things are born. Physical form is nothing but a coarser manifestation of these so-called ethers or gases."[10] Or, as an esotericist would put it, dense-physical forms are the precipitation of their etheric blueprints, which sometimes manifest themselves to people with etheric vision in the form of auras and which have been recorded on (dense-physical!) photographs through a technology developed by Semyon Kirlian. And by lowering or increasing the rate of vibration of their craft and their bodies the Space Brothers can 'drop' into or out of our range of vision at will.

Given the revolutionary and controversial nature of Adamski's claims of meeting with people from other planets, and because the reality of his contacts was in danger of being discredited by an upsurge of psychics who began to "receive messages" from the Space Brothers[11],

Adamski tried at all costs to keep the subject of the physical reality of the space people and their craft out of the field of the esoteric. He refused to make a distinction between the dense-physical and etheric-physical reality, and once told co-author Desmond Leslie, "They were not goddam spooks!"[12] Leslie, however, was convinced that Adamski "didn't want to confuse the issue"[13] because on one occasion Adamski admitted to him that "no one of us could be taken to another planet in our system and see the home world of its inhabitants in *his present bodily form or condition*."[14] For, as Benjamin Creme says, "All the planets of our system are inhabited, but if you were to go to Mars or Venus you would see nobody because they are in physical bodies of etheric matter."[15]

Leslie suggests, therefore, that Adamski's much-contended three-day trip to Saturn in 1962[16] for an interplanetary conference was "a spiritual, out of the body experience".[17] Interestingly, when asked about his own work for the Space Brothers, in the late 1950s, Benjamin Creme explained that he worked briefly with a group of which Adamski was also a member and who only met outside the body: "We did not meet in the physical body. We would not meet in a club or anything like that. Some of us knew each other on the outer plane but we did not meet as a group except out of the body."[18]

While the average person has similar experiences in dreams or other stages of sleep, everyday life on Earth is still chained to the dense-physical level, according to the Wisdom tradition, because mankind has lost sight of its oneness and must overcome its separative and materialistic tendencies through the dense-physical experience.

Matters of perception

Even if we make allowances for the political and scientific constraints given above, some issues surrounding Adamski's claims of his contacts with people from other planets and his visits to their home worlds have remained stubbornly disputed. However, seen in the context of the Ageless Wisdom teaching, against whose background Adamski's work is re-evaluated here, these too will be seen to be less confounding than some would like them to be.

The least material of these issues from our perspective is the matter of Adamski's highly detailed photographs of UFOs, which provide an argument that cannot be won from people who refuse to face the facts – for them, fuzzy photographs do not show sufficient detail to be taken seriously, while clear pictures, such as Adamski's, are too detailed to be authentic. Hence, different people assuaged their anxiety over Adamski's famous photographs of a Venusian scout ship by 'identifying' it as a street light, the top of an Italian ice-machine, or the top of a chicken brooder, to name just a few. Others had accused Adamski of photographing a lampshade, but when an identical saucer was photographed near Coniston in Lancashire, England[19], Desmond Leslie quipped "that the 'lampshade' in question must have been possessed of amazing self-propelled qualities, including the ability to fly across the Atlantic, six thousand miles from California."[20]

Since a consensus about a terrestrial explanation seems so hard to reach, perhaps there is reason to heed the verdict of experts from those pre-Photoshop days of photography. The first, J. Peverell Marley, the chief trick photographer working for famed Hollywood film director

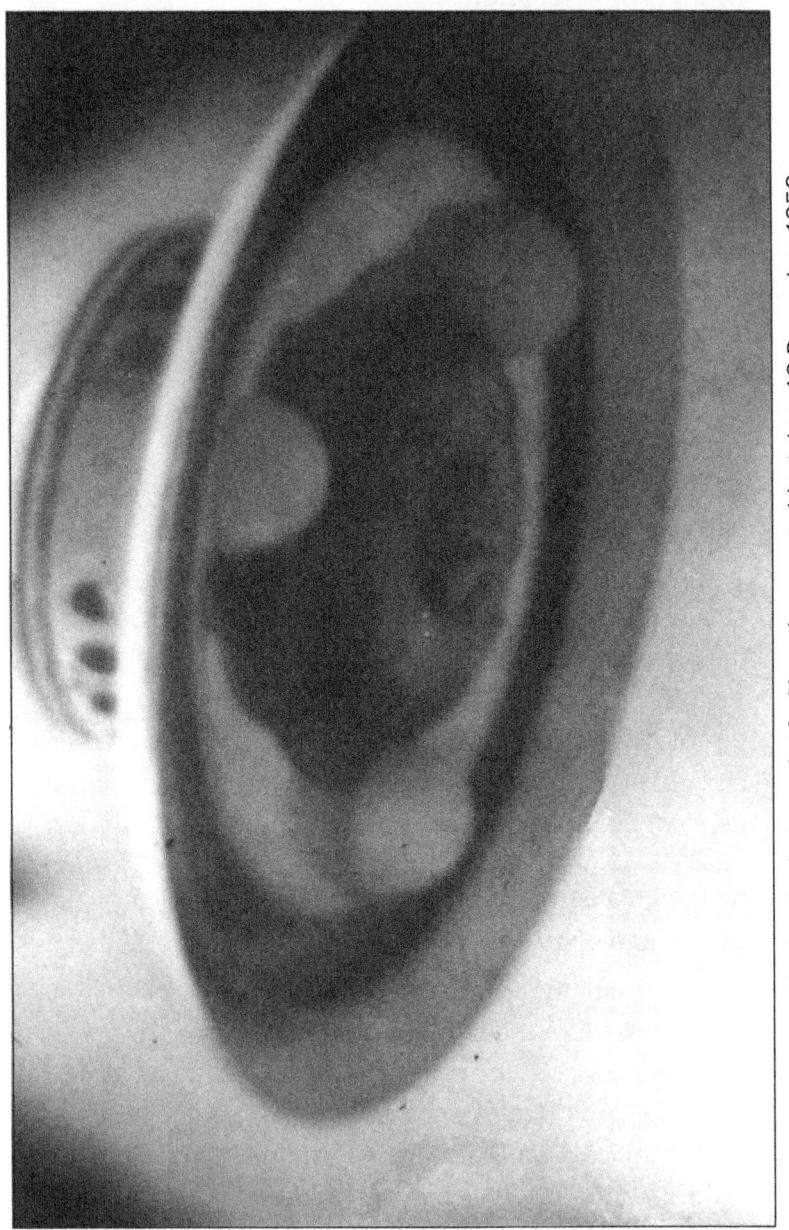

Adamski's iconic photograph of a Venusian scout ship, taken 13 December 1952.

(Permission granted by copyright holders, 2010. © GAF International/George Adamski Foundation, Vista, California, USA) and producer Cecil B. DeMille, stated that if faked, the pictures were the cleverest he had ever seen. Fourteen experts from the Rank Group, a leading British film company, concluded that the object photographed was either real or a full-scale model. About the latter possibility, chief of the English Jetex Model Aircraft company Joseph Mansour opined, upon visiting Adamski in California, that it would have been "impossible without the expenditure of a large sum of money, and doubtfully even then, to make any model resemble the strange craft" photographed by Adamski.[21]

Other issues that less than perceptive critics keep trying to use as rocket fuel for their arguments concern several instances when Adamski seemed to have contradicted himself, for instance when one of his associates saw Adamski lying in bed during the days while he was on a three-day trip to Saturn in 1962. While some of these issues had even his staunchest supporters fizzling, most of them have been dealt with intelligently, and intelligibly, by Desmond Leslie in his 'Commentary on George Adamski' which he added as Part Three to the revised and enlarged edition of *Flying Saucers Have Landed* (1970) and, even if subsequent authors chose to ignore his comments, do not need to be repeated here beyond what has been said in the preceding section.

Leslie's elaborate defence of Adamski is remarkable given that elsewhere he admitted to being disappointed that he had not been granted a meeting with a space visitor or a ride in a flying saucer. However, his unusual honesty and self-knowledge might explain why he continued to believe and support his one-time co-author: "I realized later that I was in no fit spiritual state for such an experience and had

I been taken aboard a saucer I doubt if I had been a very successful prophet afterwards, for my ego is highly susceptible to spiritual aggrandizement."[22]

It is interesting to note that Lou Zinsstag, Adamski's national contact in Switzerland, in discussing these same issues makes no reference to Leslie's Commentary in her part of the book *George Adamski – The Untold Story* (1983), which is otherwise highly informative and more of a rehabilitation of Adamski than anything else. At the same time she remarks: "From 1961 on, George kept to treatises on cosmic philosophy and cosmic science, to basic ethical issues and to Christ's teachings" which she found "too repetitive and sometimes too abstract".[23] And, "I must confess, I became tired of Adamski's articles on cosmic philosophy. They were moralizing and indulgent, and often singularly pointless I thought."[24] "[H]is printed bulletins became devoid of objective or relevant information…"[25]

Desmond Leslie, again, showed greater perceptiveness in his obituary for Adamski: "It seems very likely that George was chosen (…) to confound the intellectual and the arrogant and the know-alls, just as the prophets in the past have been chosen whose very simplicity and humble birth has made them better vehicles for a spiritual message than those whose reasoning powers have clogged up their spiritual channels."[26]

Expansions and limitations
Even a cursory glance at the lives and work of the pioneers of humanity reveals that their efforts invariably first meet with disdain, slander, and hostility from the scientific,

political and religious establishments of their time, before becoming accepted as mainstream knowledge by later generations. This holds true for Galileo, who was the first to publicly propose Copernicus' views of the actual position and relationship of the Earth to the Sun, as much as it does for H.P. Blavatsky, who introduced to mankind the notion of its spiritual heritage, the evolution of consciousness and the existence of the Masters of Wisdom as the Elder Brothers of humanity. Galileo was branded a heretic and was placed under house arrest for many years until his death, while Blavatsky was denounced by scientists and religionists alike, and dismissed as an imposter and a charlatan. She is still generally considered a 'fake', even though the Society for Psychical Research, on whose report from 1885 this condemnation was largely based, unequivocally retracted that very same report a full century later, in 1986.[27]

In many ways Adamski's work provided a similar expansion of human consciousness, by introducing to the world the reality of people inhabiting other worlds and their visits, and he had the personal experiences to show for it. Nevertheless, for many years George Adamski and his writings have been the laughing stock of the media, scientists and researchers, to the extent that even many who are convinced that UFOs exist choose not to refer to Adamski for fear of 'ridicule by association'.

Some people, like Lou Zinsstag, suspect that with regard to the controversies that arose from apparent contradictions or what many considered outrageous claims, Adamski may have been the victim of misinformation on the part of less benign extraterrestrial visitors or, alternatively, of government agents posing as space people.[28] However, in the words of Benjamin Creme, there are "unwritten laws of reticence in the Master-disciple relationship"[29], and it seems appropriate to see Adamski's relationship with his extraterrestrial contacts in much the same way, as will be shown in subsequent chapters.

Benjamin Creme also says he can vouch for the authenticity of Adamski's contacts from his own experiences, but adds: "I am pledged to silence on certain work for and with the Space Brothers".[30] Adamski was bound by similar vows of discretion and therefore found it necessary, perhaps not to contradict himself, but to express himself in ways that were open to multiple interpretations. As the Space Brothers told him: "[T]he whole of what is now permissible for you to tell cannot, with wisdom, be told to all. This is where your good judgment enters. After all, you have devoted the better part of your life to teaching universal law insofar as you knew it. In doing so, you learned well that it is not only useless, but often dangerous, to give more knowledge than can be absorbed or understood. We know that you will apply this principle to the information you receive from us."[31]

This Adamski did to the extent that he once confided to William Sherwood, an optical physicist at Eastman Kodak who examined some of his later films of UFOs, which Sherwood found absolutely authentic: "My heart is a graveyard of secrets."[32] Similarly, one of Adamski's intimates told Desmond Leslie: "If George had been allowed to tell all he knew, his life would have been much easier for him. He'd have been able to prove his case."[33]

In any case, Adamski never demanded unquestioning belief, nor did he claim infallibility. In a letter to supporters from December 1963, when even some of his closest associates had left him, he wrote: "As a man I am no different than any of you, so I am not free from making a mistake. But when I do, I correct it as soon as I can or am permitted to do so. By mistakes we learn the better way if we are big enough to admit them... I do not know all of the answers to all of the questions that may be asked of me. I know the human mind and the human purpose in this field. I am trying to help everyone who needs my help. (...) I can answer problems pertaining to humanity's purpose or cosmic destiny. ...I am limited in the mechanics of the day, but not in the mechanics of cosmic principles. So here you have my limitations."[34]

As for Adamski's personal contacts with people from our neighbouring planets, it seems safe to assume that nothing but front row seats at a mass landing and/or a personal encounter will satisfy the skeptics. The problem here could be though that, instead of inclusiveness, their attitude is informed by fear or some form of attention deficit. And while the interplanetarians appear increasingly willing to introduce themselves to people of Earth, given the growing number of testimonies that are consistent with Adamski's descriptions, both these motives seem the surest way to preclude such encounters.

Instead of setting out, then, to prove Adamski's claims by checking and validating his statements about his experiences, or disproving others' claims to the contrary, it seems more fruitful to look at the *substance* of his work – educating mankind about our essential oneness; our responsibility for our fellow man and for our home, planet Earth – with a view to the wisdom of the ages, with which the teachings of the Space Brothers cannot but coincide. For, unless we are prepared to see his work in light of the evolution of consciousness as the driving force behind the world of appearances, seeming contradictions will retain overwhelming importance, and the spiritual nature and ultimate significance of George Adamski's mission will continue to elude us long after the disinformation campaign about UFOs and the Space Brothers has proved futile.

Notes

Politics as usual:
1 Benjamin Creme (2010), *The Gathering of the Forces of Light – UFOs and Their Spiritual Mission*, p.10.
2 See for instance Alice A. Bailey (1942), *Between War and Peace*.
3 George Adamski (1957-58), *Cosmic Science for the promotion of Cosmic Principles and Truth*, Part No.1, Questions #3 and #6.
4 Adamski (1965a), *Answers to Questions Most Frequently Asked About Our Space Visitors And Other Planets*, p.28.
5 Adamski (1957-58), Part No.1, Question #9.

The problem with science:
6 "The fact that Adamski possesses more wisdom than formal education is, in his case, an asset, leaving him free of the fetters which too often shackle the academic mind." Charlotte Blodget in her Introduction to George Adamski (1955), *Inside the Space Ships*, p.11.
7 Creme (2010), pp.66-67.
8 Ibid., p.77.
9 Adamski (1957-58), Part No.2, Question #23.
10 Ibid., Part No.1, Question #12.
11 Desmond Leslie, Foreword to Adamski (1955), *Inside The Space Ships*, p.27.
12 Leslie & Adamski (1970), *Flying Saucers Have Landed*, Revised and Enlarged edition, p.250.

13 Interview with Desmond Leslie in M. Hesemann (1996), *UFOs: The Contacts – The Pioneers of Space*.
14 Leslie & Adamski (1970), p.259.
15 Creme (2001), *The Great Approach*, p.129.
16 Adamski (1962), *Special Report : My Trip to the Twelve Counsellors' Meeting That Took Place on Saturn, March 27-30, 1962*.
17 Leslie & Adamski (1970), p.258.
18 Creme (2010), pp.63-64.

Matters of perception:
19 See Leonard Cramp (1954), *Space, Gravity & The Flying Saucer*, Chapter 15. Under continued pressure from the media Stephen Darbishire, who took the photograph of the UFO near Coniston, later 'admitted' that it was a fake, but in 1986 wrote that he had said that "in desperation" (Timothy Good (1987), *Above Top Secret*, Guild Publishing, London, UK, p.373).
20 Leslie, Foreword to Adamski (1955), p.23.
21 Waveney Girvan, editor-in-chief at T. Werner Laurie publishers, Letter to the Editor of *The Observer* newspaper, October 25, 1955 (reproduced in G. Barker (ed.) (1980), *The Adamski Documents, Part I*, p.12); and Leslie in his Foreword to Adamski (1955), p.23.
22 Leslie (1965), 'A Tribute to George Adamski', *Flying Saucer Review*, July/August 1965 (as reprinted in G. Barker (ed.) (1966), *Book of Adamski*, p.11).
23 Lou Zinsstag & Timothy Good (1983), *George Adamski – The Untold Story*, p.77.
24 Ibid., p.78.
25 Ibid., p.89.
26 Leslie (1965), in Barker (ed.) (1966), p.12.

Expansions and limitations:
27 Sylvia Cranston (1993), *HPB – The Extraordinary Life & Influence of Helena Blavatsky*, p.xvii.
28 Zinsstag & Good (1983), p.88.
29 Creme (1979), *The Reappearance of the Christ and the Masters of Wisdom*, p.11.
30 Ibid., p.13.
31 Adamski (1955), p.102.
32 Interview with William Sherwood in Hesemann (1996).
33 Leslie & Adamski (1970), p.242.
34 Adamski (1965b), *Cosmic Bulletin*, December 1963, p.5.

2. The Man:

George Adamski was born on 17 April 1891 in what is now Poland as the first son of a Polish carpenter and an Egyptian mother, who had two more sons and two daughters. When he was around two years old, the family emigrated to the USA and settled in Dunkirk, New York. From 1913-1916 Adamski served in the US Army as a Private in the 13th Cavalry on the Mexican border and, from 1918-1919, in the US National Guard, Company A, 23rd Battalion. In 1917 he married Mary Shimbersky, who died of cancer in 1954. Adamski settled in Laguna Beach, California, in 1926 where he founded the Royal Order of Tibet in 1934. He moved to Valley Center near Palomar Mountain in 1940, which remained his operating base until he died of heart failure on 23 April 1965, while staying with friends in Silver Spring, Maryland. His remains are buried at the Arlington National Cemetery in Arlington, Virginia.[1]

'Who *are* you, George?'

Young Adamski
In the 1996 film documentary *UFOs: The Contacts – The Pioneers of Space* Desmond Leslie recalls how, on their last meeting in England in 1963, Adamski showed him his navel. Describing what he saw, Leslie says: "He didn't have one. He had a starburst incised in his belly, at the depth of my finger, cut into the flesh – deep, deep, deep channels. I said, 'How the *hell* did you get *that*!?' And he said, 'I don't know. I was born with that, I've always had it.' I said, 'Who *are* you, George'?"[2]

History has left us with intriguingly little information about George Adamski's early life. What little there is, however, already seems to point to his extraordinary future, and perhaps his origins.

In reference to his childhood Adamski gave Desmond Leslie a few more details: "I cannot remember anything before I was four years old when my parents, who were Polish immigrants, came to America. And they told me, while they were waiting on the docks before the ship – with a little boy of four[3], George Adamski – a mysterious man just came up and took him away. A few minutes later they brought him back again and he was a different child."

Lou Zinsstag references an early biographical sketch which states that after a short period of formal schooling (some sources say economic hardship forced him to drop out of school in the 4th grade), Adamski "was taught by private tuition". As his parents were poor and his father died when George was still a child, Mrs Zinsstag wonders how his mother could have afforded a private tutor at all. She continues: "I suspect that the young boy must have enjoyed private tuition by a teacher or guide, connected with a group in Tibet, as he subsequently founded the 'Royal Order of Tibet', and the monastery at Laguna Beach, California in the Thirties."[4]

Her suspicion is seconded by author Henry Dohan who, in his book *The Pawn of His Creator*, writes that while en route to Dunkirk, New York, the Adamski party was befriended by "a tall man with dark features" whom the author refers to as "Uncle Sid". The stranger spent "many hours in the company of young George throughout the voyage" and after their arrival, Mr Dohan continues,

'WHO *ARE* YOU, GEORGE?'

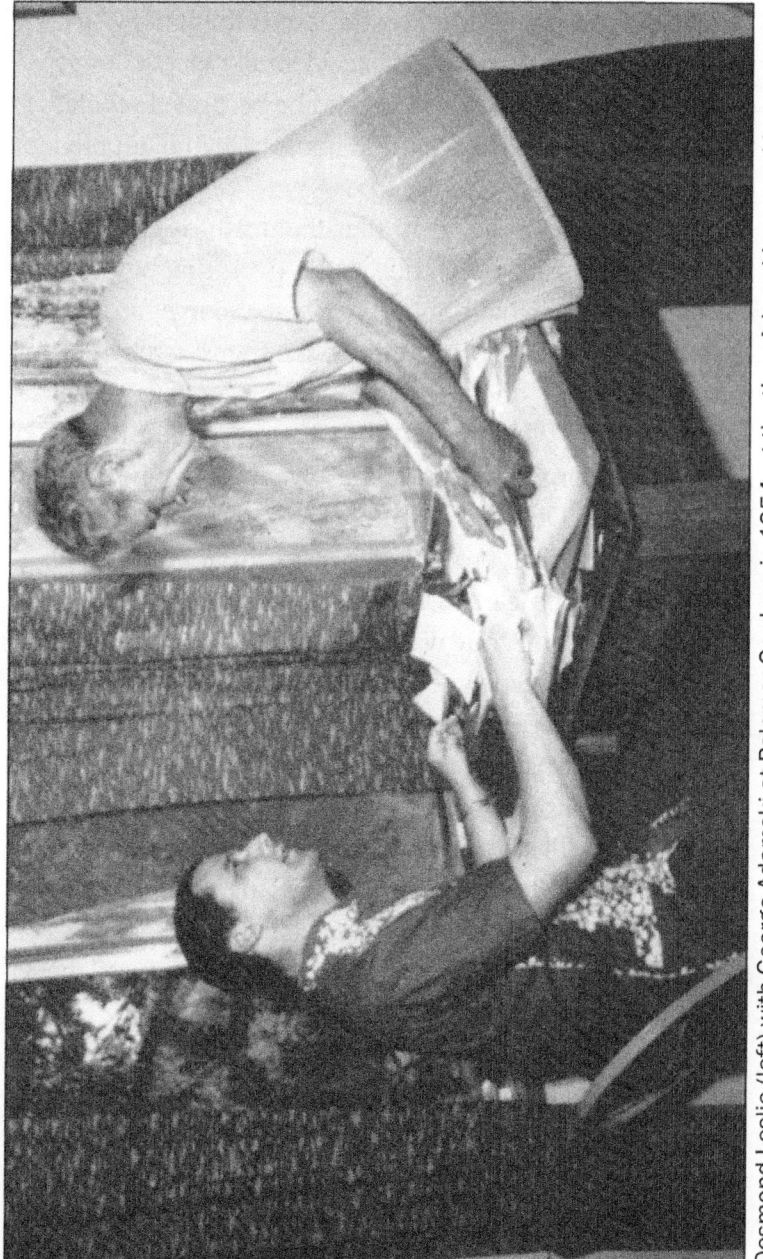

Desmond Leslie (left) with George Adamski at Palomar Gardens in 1954, at the time Adamski was working on *Inside the Space Ships*.

(Used with permission from the Leslie Estate)

"Uncle Sid remained a friend of the family for many years. On many occasions Sid would accidentally meet George on his way to and from school, and he became a regular friend and visitor to the Adamski household and adopted a godfather image to George."

Dohan also writes that after the death of George's father, Uncle Sid effectively took over the paternal responsibilities. What's more: "When George became twelve, his benevolent uncle offered the sponsorship of his further education" and suggested "sending George to Tibet to a monastery of Lamas". When Uncle Sid had finally convinced George's mother of the advantages for her son, she consented. Dohan continues: "George Adamski spent three years[5] in Tibet, probably the most important years of his life. In Tibet he learned to master the four elements: fire, water, air and earth." He was also taught the spirituality of the East and practiced meditation. According to Dohan, Adamski acquired yogic abilities and healing powers in Tibet: "The people who were around Adamski and who knew of his unusual powers were asked to keep it a secret. Adamski thought it would prejudice his prestige as a teacher, as people would take him for a magician."[6] In her book, though, Lou Zinsstag describes an example of Adamski's extraordinary powers, when he diagnosed what caused the deformity of the eye of a boy, in Rome in 1963.[7]

In 1936, ten years before he says he first sighted a flying saucer, George Adamski published his first book, containing a collection of answers to questions from his audiences as a self-described "wandering teacher" of the Royal Order of Tibet, titled *Wisdom of the Masters of the Far East*. Other than this circumstantial evidence of his association with the Masters of Wisdom, there is only one documented instance of Adamski himself referring to his experiences in Tibet, in an interview about the founding of the Royal Order. On 8 April 1934 the *Los Angeles Times* reported about the new 'cult': "Central figure in the new movement is Prof. George Adamski, sturdy, middle-aged. He is as strange as the cult he sponsors. Now he is an American citizen and served in the World War, but as a child he lived in the ancient monasteries in Tibet and learned the law of the lamas." The article goes on to quote him as saying: "I learned great truths up there on the roof of the world, or rather the trick of applying age-old knowledge to daily life, to cure the body and the mind and to win mastery over self and soul."[8]

The teachings in his first booklet cover most of the basic tenets of the Ageless Wisdom teaching, which was first introduced to the West between 1875 and 1891 by H.P. Blavatsky, who studied with the Masters in Tibet for many years herself.[9] These teachings were later expounded by Alice A. Bailey, who from 1919 to 1949 worked as the amanuensis for one of the Masters. The most recent elaborations of the Wisdom teachings are found in the books by Benjamin Creme. He states that the teachings given since 1875 are meant to prepare humanity for the return to the everyday world of the Masters of Wisdom for the first time since They withdrew to the remote mountain and desert areas when the main continent of Atlantis was destroyed 98,000 years ago. Benjamin Creme's Master has confirmed that Adamski's "Uncle Sid" was in fact a Space Brother.[10]

Adamski, the initiate

The best testimony to a man's character, if not his stature, is when his actions reflect his words. In Adamski's case this is not difficult to establish when we compare his motto, as expressed in one of his lectures, with his life: "My advice to you is to help as many as you can – the greater the number you serve, the greater will be the understanding of yourself. This should be the motive of everyone who desires to fulfill the destiny for which he was born."[11]

Robert Chapman, science correspondent for the UK *Sunday Express* newspaper, recalls his meeting in 1963 with the man in whose information he admits he was mostly interested for a sensational story: "I did not know enough about him to have formed any clear impression of the sort of man I was going to meet but, if anything, I expected an individual of obvious wealth (he must have made a packet!) and of rather hectoring, go-to-blazes manner. One would have to be, surely, to have withstood all the publicity, criticism and abuse that have been hurled at George Adamski. In the event I found a modest, soft-spoken man with a gentle, patient face, who answered every question fully and politely, without the slightest attempt at evasion or the slightest show of hostility, and who was evidently prepared to go on answering as long as I cared to put the questions. (…) If anyone believed him he was glad; if they did not it was too bad but what could he do about it? (...) I told myself that if he were deluded he was the most lucid and intelligent deluded man I had ever met."[12]

Desmond Leslie seems to agree when he reminisces: "Anyone who knew him grew to love him immensely.

'WHO *ARE* YOU, GEORGE?'

Our first contact was so strange. I had *Flying Saucers Have Landed* being rejected by publisher after publisher, when I heard, through a friend, of the first desert contact a week previously. I immediately wrote to George asking if he would let me see and possibly buy his photographs for my book. He replied by sending me the whole remarkable set of pictures, along with permission to use them for free. I thought what an extraordinary man. He takes the most priceless pictures of all time and wants no money for them. Later he sent me his manuscript humbly suggesting I might be able to find a publisher for it. By this time dear Waveney Girvan[13] had accepted my book and was perturbed that if we used George's pictures and synopsis of his story with our own, George's book wouldn't stand a chance; and after much soul searching suggested a joint publication. We wrote off to George who cabled back the following day before receiving our letter, 'Agree to joint publication.' Here indeed was telepathy at work!"[14]

Lou Zinsstag likewise notes: "Adamski's most remarkable qualities were not immediately obvious: one had to be very observant. He had a way of playing them down, as for example his devotion to his difficult task and the courage needed to fulfil it. He would rather play a light-hearted, easy-going fellow, and never spoke in public of the depth of his feelings, nor of his complete involvement in his space friends' plans."[15]

In her book Mrs Zinsstag also describes how she couldn't fail but notice how Adamski had changed greatly toward the end of their association. "I felt that he was playing the part of a contented lecturer, while concealing an inner wariness [sic],"[16] she writes about their meeting in

May 1963. This change had apparently begun to set in a few years earlier. "Adamski's co-workers had been aware for already quite a time of the heavy burden of responsibility that the work he had to carry out imposed on him, and that he was not in too good a state of health... His letters had become shorter, his statements were often unclear and everybody could feel he was under constant pressure."[17]

The Ageless Wisdom teaches that the final phase of man's evolution on planet Earth is characterized by five crises, five great expansions of consciousness, or initiations. These have been exemplified in the life of Jesus as the Birth, the Baptism, the Transfiguration, the Crucifixion (or Great Renunciation) and the Resurrection – each confirming and consolidating for the candidate his control over, successively, the physical, the astral-emotional, the mental, the personality and the soul plane of existence. At the fifth initiation, the Resurrection, man stands free as a Master of Wisdom, able to express his divine soul on the physical plane.[18]

That last part of the path of return to our Source is by no means the easiest, in some ways perhaps even more arduous and painful than the long string of incarnational experiences that leads up to it, and which we undergo in a slowly decreasing measure of blissful ignorance. Thus, the Tibetan Master Djwhal Khul (DK) says: "... an initiate is but a battle-scarred warrior, the victor in many a hard-won fight; he speaks not of his achievements, for he is too busy with the great work at hand; he makes no reference to himself or to all that he has accomplished, save to deprecate the littleness of what has been done. Nevertheless, to the world he is ever a man of large influence, the wielder of spiritual power, the embodier of ideals, the worker for humanity, who unfailingly brings results which succeeding generations will recognise."

Yet the initiate, according to the Master DK, "is seldom understood by his own generation. He is frequently the butt of men's tongues, and frequently all that he does is misinterpreted. (...) But the initiate cares not, for his is the privilege to see somewhat into the future, and therefore he realises that the force he has generated will in due course of time bring to fulfilment the plan..."[19] Seen in this light it is difficult, if not impossible, to perceive Adamski's life and work as anything other than that of an initiate of the Ageless Wisdom teaching.

Indeed, when Leslie last saw Adamski he, again, noticed a remarkable change, but to the opposite: "There was greater calmness, a heightened spirituality, and the traces of tiresome egotism that had annoyed me ten years earlier had entirely disappeared. He was one who had experienced the ultimate mysteries, and no longer cared whether he was believed or disbelieved. He knew."[20]

Over the years, through his own contact with a Master of Wisdom, Benjamin Creme has given the point in evolution, or degree of initiation, of many historical figures. According to Creme's Master, George Adamski was an initiate of the second degree.[21] This means he was mentally polarized and had therefore raised his consciousness above the astral-emotional level where the consciousness of average humanity is focused. As a personality, however, he did not yet fully identify with the soul, as would a third-degree initiate.

'Yamski', the Venusian

George Adamski was 74 when he died on 23 April 1965 (St George's Day), but the mystery that was his life did not end on that day.

In his obituary for the *Flying Saucer Review* Desmond Leslie wrote: "George claimed that many thousands of more mature souls who'd once lived on the Earth were returning both in flying saucers and by rebirth to help our planet through its time of trial. It seems very likely that George was one of them... We shall miss George. Miss him very much, but I cannot feel sad at his going. He gave his utmost to the work and the world will never be quite the same place again, richer for his coming, a little poorer for his going. But, I don't believe by any means we have seen the last of him. If he is reborn on another planet, he has promised to come back and contact us when possible. With George anything could happen. And usually does! Dear Old Space Man – Go in Peace!"[22]

Of all the claims of people having met occupants of flying saucers in the wake of Adamski's story, one stands out for its curious details. Having become the centre of attention for the local media and the British UFO community after reporting a UFO sighting on 7 June 1965 near Scoriton, Devon, UK, Ernest Arthur Bryant confessed to investigators that he had already met three "Beings from Space" on 24 April that year. As he was walking on the edge of Dartmoor, Bryant saw a "large saucer-like object" appear out of nowhere over a nearby field. The background and details of his story were described by Eileen Buckle in her book *The Scoriton Mystery – Did Adamski Return?*

In spite of his initial fear something made him stay put and when the saucer had landed and a door had slid open, he saw three figures in silver-coloured suits appear from the craft. Two of the figures had "thin and sallow" features and "extremely high foreheads which came to a point". Bryant also reported seeing only four fingers on each hand. The third person looked what he called "normal", with short brown hair and very dark brown eyes, and appeared to be between fourteen to fifteen years of age. Bryant says: "The youth appeared to be the leader of the group. He was more free and easy than the other two. 'My name is Yamski,' he said (or at least it sounded something like that). I was under the impression he was a Russian, except that he had a tendency towards an American accent, but when I asked where they had come from the reply was, 'We are from Venus.' Perhaps it was the look on my face, he turned to the others and said, 'If only Des Les were here, he would understand.' (…)

"Yamski went on to say, 'We have come to give you information. One of our reasons for contacting you is because you are of Romany origin – as am I. I have to give you a message.' It seemed that this person had been a friend of Des or Les and he wanted to tell him that only now did he realize all the work he had put into the Sanscrit [sic].[23] But he was disappointed in Des because in the last five years he had 'changed his attitude'. On saying this his eyes moistened and he turned aside as if to go inside the craft. I was wondering how it would be possible to impart this information. Yamski said, 'We will arrange that he comes to you.' (I had no knowledge then who Desmond Leslie was.) Yamski went on to say that he and these

THE RETURN OF GEORGE ADAMSKI

Before Prof. Adamski's passing, it was predicted that he would return to earth in the body of a young person to continue his great Teachings.

NOW — one of England's most famous UFO research groups has come across evidence of his return!

These findings have been published in a 325-page, fully illustrated hard cover book, titled "THE SCORITON MYSTERY — DID ADAMSKI RETURN?"

This book reveals for the first time an amazing flying saucer landing and conversation with their occupants — one of whom identified himself, for all practical purposes, as George Adamski — in the body of a 14-year-old boy!

Read how Adamski offered "Proof of Mantell" by giving the witness pieces of Mantell's crashed plane, analyzed by seven atomic physicists.

This could be the most exciting event of our century. A limited quantity of this large book has been imported, and offered to genuine seekers only. Please RUSH coupon today for your copy!

A 1968 ad announcing the availability in the US of *The Scoriton Mystery — Did Adamski Return?*

people were going to bring proof of a wonderful existence and life beyond understanding."[24]

In the event, Desmond Leslie was contacted by Mrs Buckle and her fellow researcher, who wrote to Leslie: "...as the only possible conclusion we can arrive at is that Mr Bryant was contacted by Adamski less than a day after his death and that the person referred to must be yourself, we thought it right to inform you straight away...". In his reply Leslie wrote: "Adamski always called me 'Des', seldom Desmond – and often funnier ruder names!..." He also says: "I'm sorry Yamski seemed upset that 'Des' attitude had changed. I don't think I've changed. I wrote my thesis, gave out the knowledge I had and, in the absence of further things happening to me, felt there was not much else I could do or say profitable to the cause."[25]

The episode further gains in significance in light of the fact that Mr Bryant had had no prior interest in the UFO phenomenon, other than having read about a recent sighting in Warminster, and he had not heard of George Adamski before his experience, let alone that he knew Adamski had died the day before his encounter.[26]

Another remarkable experience in the same vein was described by Giorgio Dibitonto in his book *Angels in Starships*, first published in Italian in 1983. In it he describes how, in April 1980, he saw visions of a beautiful young man who directed him to drive into the hills around Genova, Italy. He was led into a clearing in a wooded valley where he saw a UFO that had landed and was contacted by the occupants. He had regular contacts after his first encounter and on one such he was introduced to Space Brothers who called themselves Orthon and Firkon, the same names that George Adamski had used for the Space Brothers in *Inside the Space Ships*. Kalna, Ilmuth and Zuhl also join the party in Mr Dibitonto's description, while the Brother whom Adamski had referred to as Ramu, here introduces himself as Raphael.[27]

Then, the author writes, "another man was introduced to us, who impressed us immediately with his kindliness and amiability. He smiled like one who had much to say, but would not speak. 'His name is George,' said Raphael, nodding in my direction, 'the same as yours. This, our brother, lived for a while on Earth, where he chose to come on an assignment. Now he has returned to us.' We greeted one another with a warm handclasp."[28]

While the events described in *The Scoriton Mystery* sound incredible enough, it might be even more tempting to dismiss Mr Dibitonto's story as the fantasy of a man seeking publicity based on the famous story of George Adamski. Although the latter wrote of the unusual beauty, serenity and wisdom of the Space Brothers he met, he never referred to them as "angels", as Dibitonto does, whose main contact is called Raphael and whose story is infused with strong Roman Catholic references and warnings.

As was to be expected, many people dismissed Dibitonto's story out of hand. After all, the reality of which his book speaks is not conveyed through the words which the author chose to describe his experiences and the teachings which he and his companions received. Yet the reality of the interconnectedness of life on this planet with every expression of Life throughout the infinite cosmos speaks from his book in a way words alone could not achieve. Little wonder, then, that when the American publisher of *Angels in Starships*, former USAF fighter pilot Wendelle C. Stevens, had a meeting with Benjamin Creme in May 1990 the latter confirmed many of the statements in Dibitonto's book: "Mr Creme affirmed that George Adamski's contacts were real and that some of them took place in dense physical reality, just as described by Adamski himself. To a question about Adamski's contactors saying they came from Venus, Mr Creme readily replied that it was true. In fact, he added the information that there were many Venusians among us then, and even today, and that George Adamski was a Venusian spirit [soul] who had taken incarnation here for a very specific purpose, which he had fulfilled before leaving this realm in death of the physical body. According to Creme, Adamski continued in his Venusian 'light-body' after that, which does support the Scoriton story."[29]

Mystery, controversy and apparent contradictions surround the lives of many initiates. Undistracted by the fleeting riches of fame and money and undeterred by intimidation, as we shall see in the following chapter, George Adamski fulfilled his mission as a herald for the Space Brothers, broadening the horizon of many an Earthling.

Notes

Biographical note:
1 'Tibetan Monastery, First in America, to Shelter Cult Disciples at Laguna Beach', *Los Angeles Times*, 8 April 1934, as reprinted in Hukuda Takatoshi (ed.), *Scout Ship* No.4 (newsletter of GAP-Japan, Sapporo Chapter), December 1994, p.12; Tony Brunt (2009), 'George Adamski and the Toughest Job in the World' (*Secret History Part 3*); FBI file on George Adamski, FOI Case 8202030 (US Government, 1982).

Young Adamski:
2 Interview with Desmond Leslie in M. Hesemann (1996), *UFOs: The Contacts – The Pioneers of Space*.
3 In spite of Adamski's memory at this point, all the available sources seem to agree that the Adamski family left for the USA when George was two, rather than four years old.
4 Lou Zinsstag & Timothy Good (1983), *George Adamski – The Untold Story*, p.5.
5 In *Cosmic Bulletin* (June 1979, p.6) GAF president Fred Steckling states that Adamski spent six years in Tibet.
6 Henry Dohan (1995), *The Pawn of his Creator – Early Contactees of Interplanetary Visitations*, 2nd edition, 2008, pp.35-36.
7 Zinsstag & Good (1983), pp.65-66.
8 *Los Angeles Times*, 8 April 1934 (see Note 1).
9 Echoing Blavatsky's regret of ever having mentioned the Masters in her writings, Adamski later expressed his regret about having used the term 'Master' in referring to the Master from Venus whom he met during one of his trips to a mothership. See Adamski (1965a), *Answers to Questions Most Frequently Asked About Our Space Visitors And Other Planets*, p.21. Cf also page 63 in the current volume.
10 Benjamin Creme (2010), *The Gathering of the Forces of Light – UFOs and Their Spiritual Mission*, p.55.

Adamski, the initiate:
11 George Adamski [1962], 'Positive and Negative Thinking', as reprinted in G. Barker (ed.) (1966), *Book of Adamski*, p.50.
12 Robert Chapman (1969), *UFO – Flying Saucers over Britain?*, 1974 reprint, p.115.
13 The editor-in-chief of T. Werner Laurie Ltd. of London, UK.
14 Leslie (1965), 'A Tribute to George Adamski', *Flying Saucer Review*,

July/August 1965 (as reprinted in G. Barker (ed.) (1966), *Book of Adamski*, pp.11-12).
15 Zinsstag & Good (1983), p.8.
16 Ibid., p.60.
17 Ibid., p.76.
18 See for instance Alice A. Bailey (1937), *From Bethlehem to Calvary*.
19 Alice A. Bailey (1922), *Initiation, Human and Solar*, 9th printing, 1970, pp.103-04.
20 Leslie & Adamski (1970), *Flying Saucers Have Landed*. Revised and Enlarged Edition, p.259.
21 Creme (2010), p.56.

'Yamski', the Venusian:
22 Leslie (1965), in Barker (ed.) (1966), p.12.
23 This is a reference to Leslie's part in *Flying Saucers Have Landed*, a historic overview of the UFO phenomenon which goes as far back as the ancient Hindu scriptures.
24 Eileen Buckle (1967), *The Scoriton Mystery – Did Adamski Return?*, pp.61-63.
25 Ibid., pp.76-77. In his 'Commentary on George Adamski' Leslie expressed his complete confidence in Adamski's claims thus: "I have never seen or been inside a scout ship, never knowingly encountered a Visitor, but somewhere in the silence of my being is a knowledge, no greater than a grain of mustard seed, that knows without any explanation or apology, that these things are true; and that untruth is merely our inability to perceive and understand." (Leslie & Adamski (1970), *Flying Saucers Have Landed*. Revised & Enlarged Edition, p.272.)
26 Ibid., p.52 and p.82.
27 Giorgio Dibitonto (1990), *Angels in Starships*, p.13.
28 Ibid., p.30.
29 Ibid., p.iv. Mrs Buckle's fellow investigator, Norman Oliver, later decided that the Scoriton episode had been a hoax, based on a statement by Mrs Bryant that her husband had made it all up. This might have had something to do, however, with the fact that Mr Bryant had recently died when Oliver contacted his widow again and she just wanted to be left alone.

3. The Mission:

"Let us recognise and welcome the men from other worlds! THEY ARE HERE AMONG US. Let us be wise enough to learn from those who can teach us much – who will be our friends if we will but let them!"
—George Adamski, ***Flying Saucers Have Landed***

For the betterment of all

The fiction
Co-author of *Flying Saucers Have Landed* Desmond Leslie (1921-2001) was a descendent in an Anglo-Irish line of aristocrats. He was a novelist, a screenwriter (he wrote the script for the 1954 film *Stranger from Venus*) and a director, as well as a pioneer of electronic music, composing what he called 'musique concrete', and privately published the album *Music of the Future*. And while Jonathan Swift once wrote: "Here I am in Castle Leslie, With rows and rows of books upon the shelves, Written by the Leslies, All about

themselves"[1], in 1958 Desmond Leslie published a remarkable novel which was not about himself or his family. It was titled *The Amazing Mr Lutterworth*.

In the novel we first meet Mr Lutterworth while he is regaining consciousness on a liner en route from England to New York City. He is in possession of 78 tube-shaped crystals that he suspects are crucial to his mission, but an unfortunate fall during a tour of the ship prevents him from remembering what it was. Upon his arrival in New York he is persuaded to meet Hasley B. Widlow, the president of Global Oil Corporation, who offers him half a million dollars "plus royalties" for the crystals and the blueprint of a working device. As Mr Lutterworth is still at a loss, due to his amnesia, as to the nature of his mission and the crystals, he negotiates some time to consider the offer. He plans to make his way to California to meet Elias Minovsky, a curious character who lives on Mount Ramolap, writes "cockeyed philosophy that no one will publish", and makes vague photographs of flying saucers. From him Mr Lutterworth hopes to find out more about the crystals and what he is supposed to do with them.

The novel follows Mr Lutterworth as he struggles to remember his mission to save humanity from the consequences of corporate greed in the guise of Global Oil, that wants to prevent the distribution of an extraterrestrial device for the production of unlimited energy to protect its profits.

On meeting Minovsky, Lutterworth gives the following description: "First he tells me his beliefs. With direct simplicity he outlines the cyclic journey of the spirit, from its first inception in the Divine Mind, its separation and plunge into matter; its descent through different levels of being to its emergence into conscious life through a body, and through countless other bodies, upwards on the return path of perfection. He talks simply and without using tedious metaphysical terms. He speaks with a poetic and economical use of words I imagine the teachers of old must have employed when sitting out in the desert to avoid persecution for their beliefs; Minovsky hiding in a mountain forest to escape persecution for his secrets. A man unimpressed by money or earthly power is a formidable set-back to the plans of progress – particularly the progress of Hasley B. Widlow."[2]

While the story is interspersed with many such matter-of-fact references to the cosmic philosophy of Universal Law, as expounded in Adamski's book *Inside the Space Ships*, the General Assembly of the United Nations Organization – which numbered 78 members when the novel was written – is the backdrop for the grand finale of the story. It is there, at the United Nations building in New York, that Mr Lutterworth finally pierces through his self-imposed (as we discover later) amnesia, which served to protect him until he had completed his mission, and realizes he is really one of the Space Brothers who are working to save humanity.

There follows an inspiring and moving scene, when the Brother materializes in front of the General Assembly: *"I raise my arms and the gasps and babble die down. I begin to speak the words we knew and decided long ago. Each hears me in his own tongue."* As he mentally overshadows all the members of the General Assembly, the Brother fulfils his mission to inaugurate the "Time of Splendour" by distributing the crystals as the key to the salvation of the world, so that no single country or party can monopolize the extraterrestrial technology, while he conveys these words:

"This power, I tell them, shall change the face of the Earth. No more shall small groups, nor even single men, be able to rule multitudes through hunger in their bellies; for there shall no more be hunger nor want nor cold; and in time again there shall be no more disease, for as man learns to live in harmony with nature, instead of continually struggling against it, he will destroy the cause of disease."[3]

The facts

In her book *George Adamski – The Untold Story* long-time Adamski associate Lou Zinsstag writes that Leslie admitted to her in 1962 that his novel *The Amazing Mr Lutterworth* was actually "75 per cent non-fiction ... and the principal character of the plot was, of course, George Adamski".[4] A hint at this, perhaps, was given in the fact that the author dedicated his novel, among others, to "G.A.".

Although the character of Elias Minovsky is clearly modeled after Adamski (Mt Ramolap is Palomar spelled backwards), the real Adamski in this novel is the protagonist, John Hollings Lutterworth, which seems to confirm the notion that Adamski knew he was in fact a Venusian who had taken incarnation on Earth for a specific purpose, as discussed in Chapter 2. Towards Leslie Adamski had expressed his belief "that he had reincarnated from another planet through karmic reasons to give his teachings, and I find that idea quite acceptable. He believed that others, greater in the world's esteem, had also been contacted and given the same mission, but that for various reasons had refused or failed. ... He felt that he was a broken reed, but alas the only reed willing to try and play their tune. So with all his might, with his inability to write and speak good English, and the innate difficulties of being the character that he was, he set out undaunted by criticism or abuse to give the message as best he saw it."[5]

Even if *The Amazing Mr Lutterworth* does not stand among the great literary achievements of the 20th century, the novel may prove crucial to understanding Adamski's mission of informing the world about the existence and concerns of the Space Brothers, and it contains several noteworthy correspondences with Benjamin Creme's information about the return of the Elder Brothers of humanity to the everyday world.

While this is not the place to discuss the merits of Creme's information – as even less than astute observers will find it confirmed in world events that are now unfolding – it seems pertinent to point out here the remarkable similarities between these two stories that present themselves through Leslie's novel. For, already in his first book Benjamin Creme wrote that "all the Hierarchies [of Masters] in this solar system work together, and what we call U.F.O.'s (the vehicles of the space people, from the higher planets) have a very definite part to play in the building of a spiritual platform for the World Teacher, preparing humanity for this time. In fact, since the war they have played a major role in preserving this planet intact."[6] And since December 2008, according to Creme and his Master, four giant spacecraft, 'commissioned' from different planets in our solar system, have been positioned around the Earth like modern-day 'stars of

Bethlehem', to alert humanity to the emergence of the World Teacher, Maitreya, into full public view.[7]

Furthermore, it is a well-known fact that considerable forces, connected to powerful corporate and military interests, tried to undermine George Adamski's mission to inform the world of his contacts with the Space Brothers, as we shall see below. Through information given out by Benjamin Creme we know that the solution to the world's energy problems, the Technology of Light which is being developed in co-operation with the Space Brothers, will be released when humanity has had a definite change of heart and accepts the principle of sharing as the way to create trust among mankind and so abolish war and terrorism for ever. Until that time it will not be safe to trust humanity with this advanced technology for limitless energy. That change of heart, Creme has said, will begin to set in when Maitreya mentally overshadows all of humanity on the Day of Declaration, and everyone will hear Him in their own language, as He reveals His status as the World Teacher for all humanity in a worldwide television and radio broadcast and so inaugurate the new Age of Aquarius, whose keynotes are synthesis and unity.[8]

In addition to Leslie's fictitious foreshadowing of this event in his novel, it is interesting to read what Adamski had to say, in 1958, about a possible broadcast from the Space Brothers: "I have been told they are now working on a means of conversion to enable them to safely broadcast through our [radio and television] sets should such a communication become adviseable at any time. But in [the] event this ever does take place, there will be absolutely no doubt left in the mind of anyone as to the origin of the message; for it will be heard simultaneously in every tongue, and in every part of the world."[9]

According to Benjamin Creme, "[t]he Space Brothers have on this planet various people, like Adamski and others, who are used to bring the reality of the Space Brothers to the world..."[10] as Adamski did, for the first time, in his contribution to *Flying Saucers Have Landed*: "It was about 12.30 in the noon hour on Thursday 20 November 1952, that I first made personal contact with a man from another world. He came to Earth in his spacecraft, a flying saucer. He called it a Scout Ship."[11]

Adamski's claims were substantiated by six witnesses, who were with him that day and who signed affidavits sworn before notaries public. Because of Adamski's revelatory report that was added to Desmond Leslie's historical overview of the UFO phenomenon, *Flying Saucers Have Landed* became an overnight sensation when it was published in September 1953.

It was followed in 1955 by Adamski's personal account of his experience inside a mothership, where he received teachings from someone he called a Master, titled *Inside the Space Ships*. In this book he also writes about his meetings and discussions, in February and April 1953 respectively, with several of the Space Brothers whom he refers to by names that he chose himself: Orthon and Kalna from Venus, Firkon and Ilmuth from Mars, and Ramu and Zuhl from Saturn. Adamski explains: "While I want to make it very clear that the names I am introducing for these new friends are *not* their correct names, I wish to add that I have my own good reasons for choosing them, and that they are not without meaning."[12]

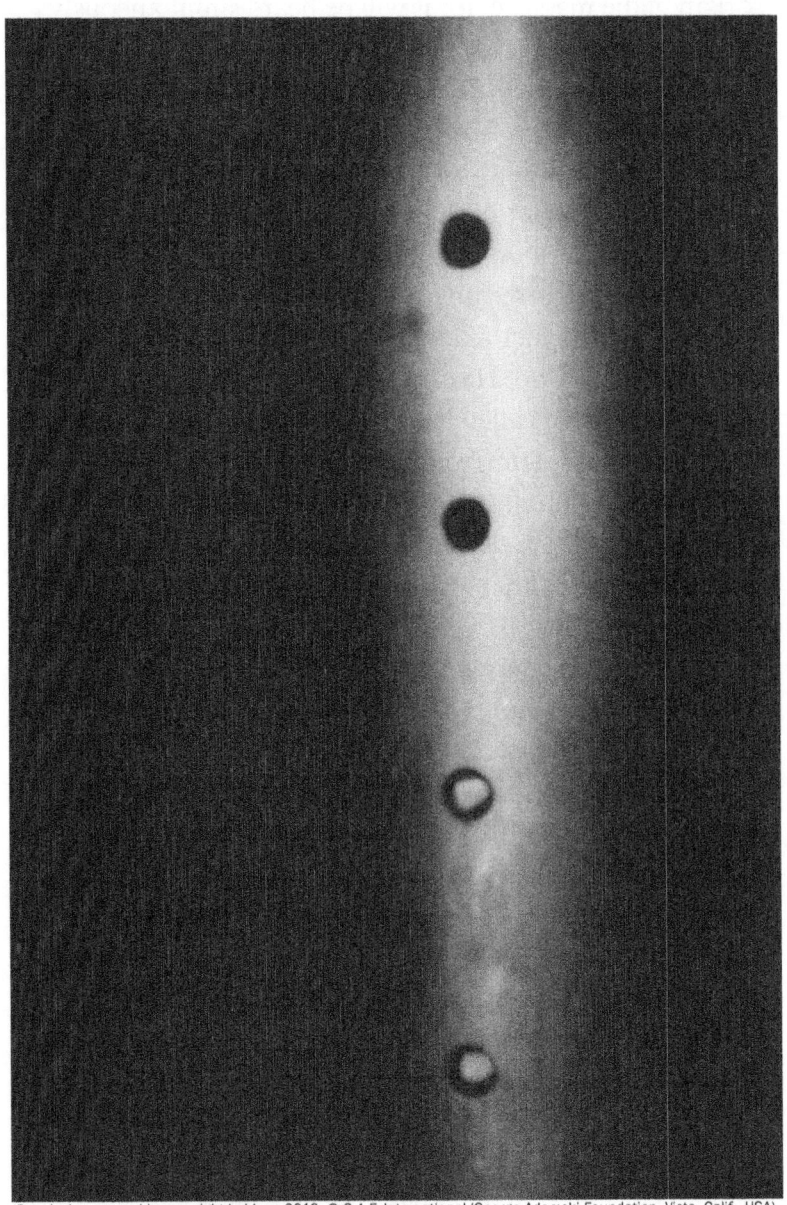

(Permission granted by copyright holders, 2010. © G.A.F. International/George Adamski Foundation, Vista, Calif., USA)

Page 44: Photograph of a mothership with Orthon and Adamski visible in the portholes, taken by a Space Brother.

In *Inside the Space Ships* Adamski describes how this photo, one in a series of four, was taken. The pilot of the scout ship who came to pick up Adamski on 24 April 1955, tells him: "This meeting has been arranged specifically to fulfill your hope of the kind of photograph you spoke of when we last met. We can guarantee nothing ... but we shall try to get a picture of our ship with you in it." (p.247) As Orthon stood in front of one porthole and Adamski in front of the one next to it, the crew "were experimenting with the amount of light necessary to show the mother ship and at the same time penetrate through the portholes to catch Orthon and myself behind them." (p.248)

Some people mistook the streak of light for a picture of the entire craft, about which Adamski says elsewhere: "One indignant skeptic, believing this to be true, even proved mathematically that in this case the portholes would be at least thirty feet in diameter, and Orthon and I would have to be giants!" He explains the physical circumstances as follows: "...there was approximately six feet between the inner and the outer portholes of this ship; forming a tunnel-like aperture. The only light available was that cast upon the larger ship by the beam sent from the scout. It was therefore necessary for this light to traverse the length of this tunnel before it could focus upon our faces. As I consider the many factors involved here, I still marvel at the ability of those men to obtain any photographs whatsoever." (*Cosmic Science* Part No.3, 1958, Question #48.)

During his meetings with the Space Brothers they made it clear that contacts had been made with the leaders of every nation, so that the coming and going of the spaceships was no secret to officialdom: "...your air forces and your governments *know* that our ships seen in your skies are from outer space, and that they can be made and piloted only by intelligent beings from other planets. Men high in the governments of your world have been contacted by us."[13]

This is a time of cosmic importance, says Benjamin Creme, as it signals the awakening of humanity from its cosmic slumber, and the Space Brothers are here to protect and help us through this period of climactic change.[14] This is corroborated by the Space Brothers themselves who tell the Italian contactee Giorgio Dibitonto of their mission to help Earth humanity in overcoming our separativeness and competition if the planet is to survive, and they ask him to inform the world of his contacts and experiences (see page 31 ff).

Dibitonto learns that the Space Brothers are now here in greater number and visibility to assist the planet in the transformation surrounding, and resulting from, the Second Coming. In reference to the Hebrews being led out of Egypt by Moses, the Space Brother named Kalna tells the author: "You will be led by a new Moses whom we all love and admire greatly. He will lead all the people on this new exodus, like a good brother or father."[15]

Just as Benjamin Creme insists that not even the Masters know the exact date when Maitreya, the World Teacher, will declare Himself openly, Adamski likewise says: "People and Nature being what they are, conditions can be altered to prevent a definite prophecy from being fulfilled. So, living moment by moment as they do, those of other worlds observe events unfolding and meet each circumstance as it arises to the best of their ability. For this reason, they make neither promises nor prophecies."[16]

Moreover, as Firkon told Adamski on their meeting in April 1953: "So long as men do not desire to change their way of living, none can help them. Those few on Earth who do sincerely desire to learn the laws of the Infinite One must try to lead the others. And we of other worlds will help them."[17]

Nuclear containment

In answer to a question (in 1958) if the space people have helped Earth humanity in any way, Adamski replies: "They have helped us in many ways of which we are little aware. To cite but a few: Any of the small conflicts that have plagued the world in recent years could have developed into worldwide destructive wars had it not been for their efforts. And the cold war which has continued for so long could have flared into open hot war had they not intervened in different ways and places.[18] Besides, they have done much to neutralize the radio-active conditions created in our atmosphere through our bomb testings. Were it not for their assistance in this, radiation would be much more pervasive than it is today."[19]

As if anticipating Benjamin Creme's notion of the spiritual mission of the UFOs as creating a platform for the reappearance of the World Teacher and helping to salvage the planet, Adamski writes: "To me, the coming of the space visitors is a holy event which should command humble respect from all. Their appearance is in accordance with the Universal Plan of brotherhood, wherein they offer a helping hand and words of counsel in time of need; a situation Earth finds itself in today."[20]

To an earlier question he answered: "Every recorded visitation from 'heaven' occurred when Earthlings found themselves in great difficulty. Then, as now, the masses were not contacted, but individuals were selected here and there. The visitors gave counsel in olden times which, when followed, revived an imperiled civilization; but when ignored that civilization eventually sank into oblivion. Today, we again stand at a momentous crossroads. The space travelers are doing their utmost to warn and help us. But the final decision lies in our hands."[21]

Earth, according to Benjamin Creme's Master, "is the most densely material of worlds and for long ages men have been in thrall to its material wealth, and have fought and competed for its control. This has brought the human kingdom (...) to the verge of destruction. With the nuclear bomb man has brought his very existence into jeopardy."[22]

Indeed it seems that whenever the Space Brothers meet with men and women of Earth, they warn against the dangers of nuclear fission technology, as they did also in Dibitonto's case. And on their first meeting the Venusian Master tells Adamski: "My son, our main purpose in coming to you [the Earth] at this time is to warn you of the grave danger which threatens men of Earth today. Knowing more than any amongst you can yet realize, we feel it our duty to enlighten you if we can. Your people may accept the knowledge we hope to give them through you and through others, or they can turn a deaf ear and destroy themselves. The choice is with the Earth's inhabitants. We cannot dictate."[23]

"Even though the power and radiation from the test explosions have not yet gone out beyond your Earth's sphere of influence, these radiations are endangering the life of men on Earth. A decomposition will set in that, in time, will fill your atmosphere with the deadly elements which your scientists and your military men have confined into what you term 'bombs'. If (...) mankind on Earth should release such power against one another in full warfare, a large part of Earth's population could be annihilated, your soil rendered sterile, your water poisoned and barren to life for many years to come."[24]

After the Master had retired Adamski asked his space friends if the drastic changes in the atmospheric conditions of Earth could be the result of the nuclear tests, to which Ramu replied: "They have indeed! And we are not guessing. Our instruments have registered those results. We KNOW!"[25] The abnormal conditions within our atmosphere of which the Space Brothers warned in *Inside the Space Ships*, have been built up within the ionosphere through the explosion of nuclear devices. "As a result, our atmosphere is being polluted (...) by the nuclear bombs that have been, and are still being, exploded around the world. This is an abnormal condition of our own making (...) only we can change it."[26]

One of the dangerous conditions that arise from nuclear tests, according to Adamski, are concentrations of radiation which at times gather together and under certain circumstances "can extract enough elements from the atmosphere as 'fireballs'. With their finer instruments, space people are able to detect these (...) pockets of radiation, visible or invisible; and when they do, they intercept and disintegrate them..."[27] Similarly, "atomic clouds that result from atomic explosions are composed of the same concentrated energy, but on a much larger scale. When an airplane flies into such a cloud it would either explode or disintegrate. With their more sophisticated instruments the Space Brothers can detect and neutralize these clouds of destruction."[28]

In his latest book, *The Gathering of the Forces of Light*, Benjamin Creme explains that our scientists do not have the technology to measure the etheric levels of energy, where the release of radiation from nuclear power plants and experimentation causes the most damage. He calls it the "deadliest release of energy that has ever taken place on Earth", which depletes our body's immune system, "causing more and more Alzheimer's, memory loss, disorientation and the gradual breakdown of our body's defence system." The Space Brothers, he says, are engaged on a spiritual mission to neutralize this nuclear radiation, spending "countless hours mopping up this energy and at the same time creating on the dense-physical plane a replica of the planet's magnetic field", through the crop circles, as part of a new energy grid that will "give this planet (...) unlimited, safe power for all purposes, in ways that cannot be bought up or cornered by any group of men."[29]

The opposition
In addition to contacting individuals, and helping mankind as a whole to minimize the damage of our dabbling with the destructive power inherent in atoms, the Space

Brothers also provided our scientists with evidence of their existence – dense-physical evidence, that is.

The crash, early July 1947, of a UFO near Roswell, New Mexico, USA, says Benjamin Creme, was a deliberate sacrifice on the part of the Martian crew, "so that we would have the evidence of the spaceship and five spacemen who could be studied and seen to be certainly similar to humans on this planet, if not identical."[30] However, after the initial reports about the facts, as far as these were known, in the evening newspapers of 8 July 1947, such as the *Roswell Daily Record,* the *Chicago Daily News*, the *Los Angeles Herald Express*, and the *San Francisco Examiner*, the morning newspapers the next day, such as the *New York Times*, the *Washington Post*, and the *Chicago Tribune*, and even the *Roswell Morning Dispatch* only carried the official denial and cover-up story about a weather balloon.

When Adamski had first met Orthon near a Venusian scout ship that had landed in the California desert near Arizona in November 1952, the *Phoenix Gazette*, of Phoenix, Arizona and the *Oceanside Blade Tribune* of Oceanside, California carried the story, and no doubt it was picked up by other newspapers. However, just as with the Roswell story, soon enough the media lost interest in the facts as they happened, and instead lent their ear to the vested interests of the military and big business.

Adamski was well aware of this unholy alliance, when he wrote to a contact in Zurich in 1955: "It is not the people who are afraid of flying saucers but all indications show that the money-pots of the world are. For, just think of the effect, once the propulsion of these ships becomes known – a power as free to everyone as the air we breathe!

What would happen to those who control the monetary system of the world? And it seems as though it were these who have put censorship on the truth, whereby publications are no longer as free as they previously were. All these branches in the media business must have money to continue."[31] In a letter to his Swiss associate Lou Zinsstag he wrote: "It is quite understandable, for the ones who control the press and all outlets of information fear the truth, so they keep it from the public the best they know how. They are the people that control the monetary system of the world, so your nation would have the least amount of information on a subject that is worldwide."[32] And during a talk at a press conference to promote his book *Inside the Space Ships*, Adamski tells his audience: "I was on Steve Allen's television show when I was in New York recently and I was told, 'Don't let anyone put words in your mouth. We've been told to play this whole thing down.' The man didn't say *who* told him."[33]

As for the government's reluctance to share their knowledge with the public, Adamski seemed willing at first to give their motives the benefit of the doubt when he said, according to Mrs Zinsstag: "...they think it wiser to let the truth come out slowly, in small amounts, so that the general public as well as industry could assimilate it more easily."[34] Alternatively, he may have made a deliberate distinction between the US government and the Pentagon (or governments and the military in general). Although it would be difficult to untangle the influence of big business from the government's (or rather, the Pentagon's) attempts to disinform, confuse or scare the public about the reality of the UFO phenomenon without exhaustive research – and perhaps such research has already been undertaken and published by authors more concerned with proving the validity of sightings and other evidence – there is no doubt that Desmond Leslie's fictitious Hasley B. Widlow and Global Oil were based on a good level of factuality.

Whoever they were, some people were already sufficiently alarmed after the publication of Adamski's first book, and offered him $25,000 if he would refrain from publishing a reprint of *Flying Saucers Have Landed* and sign a statement saying that his part of the book was pure science-fiction. In his article '*Who* is trying to stop the truth coming out?', which he wrote for the *Flying Saucer Review* (FSR) in January 1959, Adamski relates how Frank Scully, author of *Behind the Flying Saucers*, had received the same offer[35], while Lou Zinsstag reports how a friend in France uncovered an operation in which nearly the complete French edition of Scully's book had been collected and brought to a paper mill. Adamski himself had received another offer of $35,000, during a visit to Detroit, if he would change the status of his book *Inside the Space Ships* from non-fiction to science-fiction.[36]

In Switzerland, on his world lecture tour, Adamski became the target of organized disruption during his second lecture in Zurich, on 29 May 1959. In the chapter 'The Zurich Incident' in *Flying Saucers Farewell*, Adamski describes this episode, where 300 students among an audience of 700 carried out a carefully prepared plan to disturb the showing of the film by shining torch lights on the screen, clapping and stamping after every sentence and finally throwing fruit into the audience and at Adamski and his associates on the stage. All the while, a contingent of the Zurich police was present in the audience after the chief of police had requested, and had been granted, a private viewing of Adamski's film beforehand, but they had all shown up in plain clothes and did nothing to stop the students from disturbing the proceedings. A student who later came to him to offer an apology revealed that the group had been told Adamski would be discrediting a Swiss scientist in his lecture.[37]

Looking back at the events, Adamski wrote, "the picture became increasingly clear. The private viewing of my film by the police chief, the lack of cooperation from the police at my lecture, and the powerful lights thrown on the screen to prevent the public from seeing the rest of my pictures, all added up to one thing. The overwhelming onslaught of truth apparently had the 'Silence Group' greatly worried..."[38]

In the aforementioned article in FSR Adamski said: "The reasons behind this opposition are undoubtedly many. Careful analysis reveals the foremost unquestionably being the advanced reforms which could be given to the world once officials acknowledge the coming of the visitors in friendship. These people are in a position to guide us along the right path in our quest to harness the free powers of space; not alone for the propulsion of space ships, but of more importance to the average citizen, for domestic use. Think what this would mean to humanity. But while contemplating this idealistic state, do not overlook the havoc that would be created as power companies, world-wide oil interests, and kindred big businesses become obsolete..."

Similarly, in an article entitled 'My Fight with the Silence Group', he wrote: "...I wonder if Wall Street might be the central faction behind all the battling to keep the phenomenon of interplanetary visitation in the field of the occult, and combating those of us who know and announce that the space people are physical beings, travelling in mechanical space craft..."[39]

The effect of the wholesale repression of the facts is that the general public began to fear the UFOs and the purpose for their visits. Adamski understood how the game was played, when he said: "As for the governments ... whether it be this one [the US government] or any other ... you cannot look to them and expect to get the *truth*. They *have* it! But, they cannot give it. First the people must be educated. WHAT PEOPLE DO NOT UNDERSTAND ... THEY FEAR!"[40]

The spreading fear was not just a side effect of governments being unwilling – or not being allowed – to inform the people of what they knew. It was also actively engendered by some government agencies who wanted to depict the UFOs and the Space Brothers as malicious 'aliens' by repeatedly planting stories of mutilations, abductions and related aberrations. Adamski eloquently countered these defamatory attempts when he said: "To me it is sacrilegious and blasphemous to the Creator to presume we are the images of His being, then promote freaks in His name as inhabitants of other planets. The story of creation is Universal – not confined to our small planet, Earth."[41]

The reach

In the face of such formidable opposition it is all the more remarkable what Adamski managed to achieve in educating the public about his contacts and their teachings, long before the advent of the Internet and e-mail.

His approach was as modest and sensitive as that of the space visitors in their craft, showing themselves to individuals when they see an opportunity, leaving people alone when they react with fear, and leaving silent 'visiting cards' in the form of crop circles for many decades – allowing all kinds of attention seekers to claim authorship of their breathtaking designs.

While his books took the world by storm, Adamski's information about his contacts was not without precursor, even if it presents itself just as modestly. For instance, Lou Zinsstag has said that there were certain facts which led her to think that Adamski had had contact with the space people long before his reported first encounter with Orthon in 1952 – "of which meeting he could not or was not allowed to speak later."[42]

Of course there was the Space Brother known as "Uncle Sid" who arranged for Adamski's training with the Masters in Tibet[43], but it seems that Adamski only became aware of his own extraterrestrial origins at some point in his adult life.[44] Zinsstag doesn't state all of the facts that she alludes to, but it is revealing to note that eight years before Adamski says he first saw a flying saucer (which was 1946), he already installed his six-inch long-range telescope at the Temple of Scientific Philosophy, the home base for the Royal Order of Tibet in Laguna Beach. So while he was still lecturing, in the late 1930s, on Universal Law, a report in the *Los Angeles Times* in April 1938 quotes him as explaining the purpose of the telescope being "to create an interest in the study of astronomy in conjunction with other scientific subjects".[45]

When exactly Adamski became aware of his Venusian origins we do not know from existing sources, but we do know that in 1946, the year of his first saucer sighting, Adamski wrote a pamphlet titled *The Possibility of Life on Other Planets*, while in 1949 he published *Pioneers of Space – A Trip to the Moon, Mars and Venus*, in which he endeavoured to "reasonably speculate about such inhabitation of other planets".[46] And while critics have made much of some of the descriptions in this book being similar to certain parts in *Inside the Space Ships*, with our current knowledge it only makes sense that he would have presented his knowledge or undisclosed earlier experiences as fiction in *Pioneers of Space* to test the public reaction to the idea of life on other planets.

A similar simplicity and discretion of approach has been widely documented in the attempts of the Spiritual Hierarchy of Earth to awaken humanity to Their reality and was also strikingly phrased by the Space Brother called Raphael (Ramu), as recorded in Giorgio Dibitonto's book *Angels in Starships*: "Our weapons are love, discretion, wisdom and patience. We are, nevertheless, far more effective in accomplishment than you could possibly imagine. We will not allow evil to take root in the cosmos, where harmony, love, and the life-force reign. (…) Soon your planet will comprehend this too, and the long awaited day will dawn for you. I tell you truly, it will be soon."[47]

On his first meeting with a Master on a Venusian mothership in February 1953, Adamski was told: "I think the peoples of Earth would be amazed to find how swiftly change could come throughout the planet. (…) So with receptive minds and hearts everywhere on your planet, it is not too late. But there is urgency, my son! So go forth

Vol. I, No. 10   THE VISI.

GEORGE ADAMSKI IN DETROIT JUNE 29, 1957

George Adamski, well known to saucer fans throughout the world, author of 'Flying Saucers Have Landed,' and 'Inside Space Ships' will talk at the Federation of Women's Club Building, Second at Hancock, in Detroit on June 29, 1957 (Saturday) at 8:00 P.M. Mr. Adamski will be sponsored by the Interplanetary Foundation of Detroit. Tickets will be available at the door the night of the lecture. If you plan on hearing Adamski, come early...only 350 tickets printed and we understand most have been already sold!

Adamski will show a film (movie) which he states will contain shots of Flying Saucers including one of a monitoring disc which he took pictures of in Mexico enroute to California by auto. The film will also contain an interpretation of the Venusian footprints as written about in his first book, 'Inside Space Ships.'

Saucer fans in this area expect Adamski to unveil his new program here in Detroit. The program reportedly is one that Adamski received from one of his space contacts...it centers around an idea of establishing a school of instruction on Universal Law.

Adamski is also expected to attend the Michigan Flying Saucer Assembly earlier that afternoon, also at the Federation of Women's Club Building.

*****

Speculations about Adamski's "new program" which he "received from one of his space contacts..." appeared in an announcement for his lecture in Detroit on 29 June 1957 in *The Visitor* (May-June 1957), the official bulletin of Interplanetary Relations, "an informal civilian UFO research group" in the Detroit area and member of the Michigan Flying Saucer Federation. This is likely the earliest reference to the Get Acquainted Program, whose establishment was announced by Adamski in a letter dated 15 July 1957.

with the blessing of the Infinite Father on your mission, and add your voice to those of others who also carry this message of hope."[48]

As his story captivated the world following the publication of his books, Adamski was asked to give lectures around the globe, with invitations flooding in from as far afield as South America, Europe, Australia and New Zealand. Likewise, readers of *Flying Saucers Have Landed* and *Inside the Space Ships* inundated Adamski with questions. In answer to one of these he wrote, in April 1958: "The [space] visitors have made themselves inconspicuous while on Earth, conforming rigidly to our customs; for they are aware many people still find it hard to believe advanced human beings surround us in space. They are cognizant of the ridicule those whom they contact must face, yet it is imperative that certain truth be given to the people of the world at this time. As stated in *Inside the Space Ships*, I serve merely as a liaison to bring these messages to as many as I can reach."[49]

Around 1956 or 1957 the Space Brothers suggested that an international network of correspondents be established, which Adamski named the Get Acquainted Program (GAP).[50] In a letter to his associates around the world, dated July 15, 1957, Adamski explains: "To help in this movement they have suggested that I ask the help of one or more men and women in each nation, people who have proven their interest and sincerity. In turn, these leaders will need the cooperation of many others throughout their nation. Those in each locality who have already expressed an interest in our interplanetary visitors are to be made acquainted with one another. (…) Regular group meetings of such friends wherever possible are recommended for discussions and closer friendship toward greater understanding of one another.

"Information of the Brothers of other worlds, with whom I continue having more or less regular meetings, will be sent regularly to each national leader, who in turn will forward it to all of his assistants. They then will pass it on to their associates. The idea is that the citizens of each nation, through these efforts, will grow into closer united friendship with their countrymen, without discrimination or divisions of any kind. In time it is hoped that these national efforts will overflow into worldwide understanding and friendship. Suggestions will also be made monthly, for individual study and efforts toward a greater understanding of oneself, his purpose of being, his relationship to his fellowman, and his place in the Cosmos – of which we are all citizens."[51]

While his 1959 world speaking tour took Adamski to the countries where GAP chapters had been or were being established, his books had already reached a huge audience. First published simultaneously in the USA and the UK in September 1953, *Flying Saucers Have Landed* had seen six reprints by December and within three years had been reprinted 12 times in the USA alone. It was also serialized in magazines and translated into over half a dozen languages.[52]

Notwithstanding the efforts of governments or the military to undermine Adamski's claims and the benign intentions of the Space Brothers, the Get Acquainted Program proved remarkably viable, with chapters having sprung up in at least seventeen countries in Adamski's lifetime. The most successful chapter, the Japanese, which was established in 1961 by Hachiro Kubota, still counted about 1700 members among 17 local branches in 1995. It published a widely read quarterly magazine that was also sold in kiosks in major cities, as well as an annual international edition in English.[53]

But the space people measure effectiveness in rather different terms and the beauty of their approach was evinced in what they taught Adamski: "[E]very individual is a radiating center, influencing all whom he meets; and they in turn, pass on their reactions through contacts with countless others. In this way, a personal emotion can encircle the globe."[54] Lou Zinsstag quotes an anonymous article whose author comments: "Adamski was told by one of the space people: 'What you have learned can be of great value to the people of your planet. Speak to them by word of mouth and by the written word.' This Adamski did with tremendous enthusiasm and efficiency. Even those who refuse to believe him admit that his message reached an incredibly large audience."[55] And although it would be difficult to establish a direct connection with his work, it is noteworthy that the first popular anti-nuclear movement (the Campaign for Nuclear Disarmament) was formed in the United Kingdom in 1957.

The immense success of his books did nothing to distract Adamski from the simplicity of his approach. In his *Cosmic Science* bulletin Adamski describes how "on the first and third Sundays of each month, between the hours of one and four p.m., it is my custom to talk with the public at my home; give a lecture on topics of interest and answer questions."[56] He always remained true to this and practiced

GET ACQUAINTED PROGRAM LEADERS October 1959

Bauer, Mrs. Dora
Karolinengasse 14/14
Vienna IV AUSTRIA

Buhler, Dr. Walter
Rue Joaquim Nabuco 125, apt 210
Copacabana
Rio de Janeiro, D.F.
BRAZIL

Maitra, Dr. S. K.
Quarters No. D/8
Banares Hindu University
Benares 5, INDIA

Schumann, Mr. Neil
& Dr. Med. H. Büttner
Berlin-Lankwitz
Seydlitzstrasse 6 III
GERMANY

d'Aquila, Miss May
BeeklaAn 431
The Hague, HOLLAND

Kubota, Mr. Hachiro
Furukawa Street
Masuda, Shimane
JAPAN

de Rueda, Mrs. Maria Cristina
Thiers 61
Eva Angures
MEXICO D.F.

Dickeson Mr. F. W. G.
33 Dee Street
Timaru,
NEW ZEALAND

Winfelaar, Henk J. Mr.
P. O. Box 7
Henderson
NEW ZEALAND

Einsatag Miss Lou
Nedelberg 31
Basel
SWITZERLAND

Fly, Mr. & Mrs. Bill
1700 - 22nd Street
Hondo, Texas
UNITED STATES

Rickers, Cyril S.
136 Main Street
Port Dalhousie, Ontario
CANADA

Cayt, Peterson K. S.
Fraesteguardavej 40
Vejene
DENMARK

Perego, Dr. Alberto
Via Ruggero Fauro 43
Rome, ITALY

Kulenkamp, Miss Erica
Hamburg-Gross Flottbeck
Bellmannstr. 23
GERMANY

Dr. Francesco Volimeni
Via Fezzan 53
Rome, ITALY

Anstee, Mr. Ronald W. J.
8952 Jeanne Mance
Montreal P. Q.
CANADA

Wegener - Maser, Frau Ilse
Berlin-Lichterfelde
Waltoper Platz 6
GERMANY

Russell, Mr. & Mrs. Ray
P. O. Box 35
North Quay, Brisbane
AUSTRALIA

Otley, J. Leslie A. R. F. S.
41 Deanham Gardens
Fenham - Newcastle - upon Tyne 5
ENGLAND

Benjamin, Mr. Glyn T
Surveyor Generals Dept
Box 8099 Causeway
Southern Rhodesia
AFRICA

Zaleski - Mr. Kazimierz
Warszawa - 97
Post Box No. 1
POLAND

This October 1959 contact list for the Get Acquainted Program shows 22 main contacts in 17 countries: Australia, Austria, Brazil, Canada (2x), Denmark, England, Germany (3x), Holland, India, Italy (2x), Japan, Mexico, New Zealand (2x), Poland, Southern Rhodesia (now Zimbabwe), Switzerland, and the United States.

the precepts of the Brothers: "I have said many times that all of the people should know the truth and not just the 'show type' that organized at first in various groups and limited the knowledge to the few. This is why I have never organized or joined any organization for I feel the truth belongs to all classes of people."[57]

Indeed, it seems that 'organizing' efforts of a spiritual nature and the subsequent tendency to ascribe authority to people holding offices in an organization, presents a serious impediment to their efficiency. Both Adamski and the Space Brothers always emphasized the need to apply and live the teachings of our own free will. "We cannot dictate," say the Space Brothers[58]; "they only want to help us – if we will but listen and accept their help," says Adamski.[59] Likewise, about the group which Benjamin Creme formed in London in 1974, his Master said: "There should be no officers so that there would be no one in charge, no one whose word would be taken as the only arbiter in the group."[60] The Tibetan Master Djwhal Khul expressed it thus: "The sole authority is the teaching, and not the teacher; upon the rock of authority many schools have foundered. There is but one authority – each man's own immortal soul, and that is the only authority which should be recognized."[61]

Just as true effectiveness of any spiritual mission has little to do with quantity, or organisation, neither has it to do with being able to tell when the effects will become visible or known: "[S]pace people use neither position nor name to identify them [sic]. These are personality. Nor do they ever prophesy our future. They may tell us of logical results from continued actions in a certain direction, but they will never set a time. They know an infinite number of conditions can intervene to change the course of events."[62]

As was to be expected, most GAP chapters withered with the demise of Adamski or their founders and the ongoing onslaught on Adamski's character and credibility by the vested military and industrial interests, with only two European chapters holding on to a marginal existence in 2009. The Japanese chapter existed until the death of its founder in 1999, with the Yokohama branch continuing its activities under another name (Cosmic Consciousness). However, the fact that Adamski's Collected Writings in Japanese[63] was updated with a twelfth volume in 2004 shows that the power of the message which he brought endures, even without an authority or organization to represent it.

Adamski himself may have given another, related reason for the difficulty of keeping the GAP efforts going, when he said: "I can assure you of one thing, the space people are not coming merely to satisfy our personal curiosity. At the present time, I have been told, the best way we can help is by beginning to live with more respect toward one another. For as this is done throughout the world, fear and hostility between the peoples will diminish; leaving a fertile field in which to work for the betterment of all. But final success in this depends upon each individual."[64] To which he added elsewhere: "... to live this new kind of life among the many who do not, one must have unshakable faith and patience in order to endure. For not everyone will grasp the idea immediately, humanity is slow to change. But it must change if it is to survive. And pioneers in any field must be strong and determined if good results are to be realized."[65]

It is clear then, that the teachings which Adamski received through his contacts with the Space Brothers require exactly the kind of discipline and steadfastness that their herald showed in his endeavours.

Notes

The fiction:
1 Castle Leslie History website (http://www.celticcastles.com/castles/leslie/history.htm), retrieved 28 December 2009.
2 Desmond Leslie (1958), *The Amazing Mr Lutterworth*, pp.106-07.
3 Ibid., p.202.

The facts:
4 Lou Zinsstag & Timothy Good (1983), *George Adamski – The Untold Story*, p.78.
5 Leslie (1965), 'A Tribute to George Adamski', *Flying Saucer Review*, July/August 1965 (as reprinted in G. Barker (ed.) (1966), *Book of Adamski*, p.10).
6 Benjamin Creme (1979), *The Reappearance of the Christ and the Masters of Wisdom*, p.206.
7 Creme (2010), *The Gathering of the Forces of Light – UFOs and Their Spiritual Mission*, p.81 ff.
8 Ibid., p.128.
9 George Adamski (1957-58), *Cosmic Science for the promotion of Cosmic Principles and Truth*, Part No.3, Question #51.
10 Creme (2010), p.36.
11 Leslie & Adamski (London, 1953), *Flying Saucers Have Landed*, p.185.
12 Adamski (1955), *Inside the Space Ships*, p.43.
13 Ibid., p.99.
14 Creme (2010), p.13.
15 Giorgio Dibitonto (1990), *Angels in Starships*, p.33.
16 Adamski (1957-58), Part No.5, Question #88. See also Note 61.
17 Adamski (1955), p.117.

Nuclear containment:
18 See also Creme (2010), p.10-12, where he describes in more detail several ways in which the Space Brothers have intervened to avert nuclear conflicts.
19 Adamski (1957-58), Part No.2, Question #26.
20 Ibid., Part No.4, Question #64.
21 Ibid., Part No.3, Question #49.
22 Benjamin Creme's Master, 'The end of darkness', *Share International* Vol. 24, No.6, July/August 2005, p.3.
23 Adamski (1955), p.91.
24 Ibid., pp.91-92.
25 Ibid., p.98.
26 Adamski (1957-58), Part No.4, Question #73.
27 Ibid., Part No.2, Question #27.
28 Ibid., Questions #27 and 28.
29 Creme (2010), pp.13-14.

The opposition:
30 Creme (2001), *The Great Approach*, pp.133-34.
31 Zinsstag & Good (1983), p.44.
32 Ibid.
33 Adamski (1974 reprint), *Many Mansions*, pp.5-6.
34 Zinsstag & Good (1983), p.28.
35 Ibid.
36 Ibid., p.86.
37 See Adamski (1961), *Flying Saucers Farewell*, pp.160-69.
38 Zinsstag & Good (1983), p.42.
39 Adamski (n.d.), 'My Fight With The Silence Group' (as reprinted in Barker (ed.) (1966), p.34).
40 Adamski (1974), p.6.
41 Adamski (1957-58), Part No.2, Question #20.

The reach:
42 Zinsstag & Good (1983), p.19.
43 See Chapter 2, pp.20-23.
44 Creme (2010), p.39.
45 'Long-Range Telescope Added to Laguna Project', *Los Angeles Times*, 30 April 1938.
46 Adamski (1949), *Pioneers of Space*, p.2.
47 Dibitonto (1990), p.26.
48 Adamski (1955), pp.94-95.
49 Adamski (1957-58), Part No.3, Question #52.

50 Adamski (1961), pp.122-23.
51 Daniel Ross (ed.), *UFOs and Space Science*, No.1, December 1989, p.20.
52 Within a few years it had been translated into Danish (1955), Dutch (1954), French (1954), German (1954), Japanese (1954), Norwegian (1954), Portuguese (1957), and Swedish (1957), and later also in Italian (1973) and Spanish (date unknown).
53 Hachiro Kubota (ed.), *UFO Contactee* (GAP-Japan Newsletter, International Edition) No.10, February 1995, p.12.
54 Adamski (1957-58), Part No.5, Question #99.
55 Zinsstag & Good (1983), p.92.
56 Adamski (1957-58), Part No.4, Question #69.
57 Adamski (1965b), *Cosmic Bulletin*, December 1964, p.13.
58 Adamski (1955), p.91.
59 Adamski (1957-58), Part No.5, Question #89.
60 Creme (2002), *The Art of Cooperation*, p.86.
61 Alice A. Bailey (1936), *A Treatise on the Seven Rays, Vol.I: Esoteric Psychology*, Vol.I, 10th printing, 1979, p.112.
62 Adamski (1957-58), Part No.1, Question #15. See also Creme (2010), pp.83-84, where he describes man's free will to act, or not, as an inhibiting factor in setting definite dates for future events.
63 Published by Chuo Art Publishers, Tokyo, Japan.
64 Adamski (1957-58), Part No.2, Question #23. Cf Maitreya's call for sharing in order to create justice so that the trust thus engendered will allow humanity to abolish war and create peace. (See, for instance, Creme (2007), *The World Teacher for All Humanity*.)
65 Adamski (1964), *Science of Life* study course, Lesson Six: 'Newness, The Rejuvenator Of The Mind'.

4. The Teaching:

"The way may be pointed, but each must travel it for himself."
  –George Adamski, ***Flying Saucers Farewell***

Universal brotherhood, individual responsibility

Some thirty years after he studied with the Masters of Wisdom in Tibet, George Adamski published his first compilation of wisdom teachings at around age 45, titled *Wisdom of the Masters of the Far East* (1936).

In the course of Earth's history, the Masters have evolved into the next kingdom beyond the human, the spiritual kingdom, by learning to live according to the universal Laws of Life. They are the Custodians of the wisdom teaching, which They pass on in the measure that humanity is capable of absorbing, understanding and applying it, but increasingly so since 1875 in preparation for Their return to the everyday world at this time of transition.

In support of this climactic event, the Space Brothers are coming to our planet to help humanity make this transition into a higher state of consciousness, where we will become aware of the spiritual dimension of life, as exemplified by the Masters who will be living and working among us as our Elder Brothers, and the presence of the Space Brothers themselves. In the process we will also rid ourselves of the sense of separation that has brought our civilization to the precipice, and realize our essential brotherhood. What is more, we will be able and willing to put that realization into practice.

Teachings of the Masters of Wisdom
The teachings for the New Age coming from the Masters of Wisdom have been known about on a relatively large scale and have been available ever since the seminal works in this field were published by Mme Blavatsky. The teachings of the Space Brothers, however, have been largely ignored as a result of the character assassination committed on their main proponent, George Adamski. Yet, while convinced that the claims of Adamski and others about contacts with extraterrestrials "do not stand up to the slightest scrutiny", in his paper 'Meaningful Contact: George Adamski and the Contactees as Social Reformers' A.J. Gulyas recognizes more of the true scope of Adamski's teaching than most skeptics when he writes: "Adamski was one of the first to use the vehicle of the UFOs to push an agenda of widespread societal change".[1]

But before we take a closer look at the teaching of our Brothers from space, it seems appropriate to see what Adamski taught as a lecturer on oriental philosophy in the 1920s and 1930s, the better to appreciate the extent to which the teachings from the Space Brothers correspond with those of the Masters, our Elder Brothers.

In answer to the question 'What is the law of cosmic brotherhood?' Adamski wrote: "Universal love, harmony, unity, the oneness of all things. We are one with everything in the universe, every atom, every grain of sand, every flower, every manifestation either visible or invisible. God is in everything and everything is in God. (...) [I]t is the law of life, of being, of creation – God. As God is everything in the universe, and manifestations differ only in forms and degrees of manifestation, cosmic brotherhood would have to be an unchangeable, indisputable fact. There is only one cause, the Father."[2] In other words, do unto others as you would have them do unto you, because harming another is tantamount to harming yourself. The law behind this inescapable mechanism, the law of cause and effect, is the law that governs the universe.[3]

Having transgressed this universal law as much as humanity has on this planet, we have become accustomed to thinking of 'law' as something which we need to keep ourselves in check against each other. But, according to Adamski, "[law] is the positive principle of action. In the universal sense it is Primal Cause, the absolute and immutable principle of Truth or Reality which governs all motion and manifestation."[4] So as long as we live according to the Law, we act and create; when we live outside the law, not heeding the interrelatedness of everything and everyone, all we do is react and suffer the consequences of our deviation under the law of cause and effect: "Law exists; man cannot change it or overcome it, he can merely become aware of it and use his God-given wisdom in working with it to bring forth perfection, or exert his strength against it to bring forth inharmony [sic] and destruction. The law itself remains unchanged."[5]

"The law of attraction is the magnetic principle of the universe, the Soul quality of Being. The Master Jesus expressed this principle as the law of love."[6] The Masters, taught Adamski, "use the law of Love, which unites all in oneness. They do not resist anything, but take it into the love of the universe, separating nothing from the all, from the lowest to the highest. Love is the Cosmic secret of the universe, if there were any secrets, but nothing is hidden or kept in love, as it is all inclusive."[7]

For the limited size of his first booklet, a good portion of it is devoted to space and the universe. The Universe, according to Adamski's early teaching, "is the all in all – all planets of all solar systems, all chemicals from the highest invisible states to the lowest solidified forms, all vibrations, all intelligence, all consciousness. Or, in other words, the entirety of God in its various manifestations that compose the perfect Whole."[8] God, he says, is the conscious motivating force of all life. In the universe God expresses itself as Natural Law, "the directing consciousness", in man as universal thought or consciousness. "They are all the same and are one, only expressed in different words according to the labels that man has created. And man has become lost in the words, losing sight of the oneness of consciousness."[9]

UNIVERSAL BROTHERHOOD, INDIVIDUAL RESPONSIBILITY

The 6-inch telescope with which George Adamski is pictured here at Palomar Gardens circa 1954...

According to Adamski there are only two things in the universe – force (the invisible) and form (the visible)[10]. Consciousness, he explains, "is the life force of all forms. It is that which sees, hears, and feels through the senses. When consciousness leaves the body, the person is pronounced dead. But consciousness is everlasting and universal. Mortal consciousness is awareness of self as form, separate from the whole. Universal consciousness is awareness of all things as one."[11] Consciousness, then, is the aspect which moulds all the visible forms from the invisible essence of God, "first in the invisible state and then gradually bringing it into a state of greater density through a descension [sic] of vibration in the composing elements until it is finally brought into the extreme coarse state of vibration known as visible manifestation."[12]

From this incomplete summary of Adamski's early teaching it is clear that the notion of the fundamental unity of everything that exists has been central to his world view from the outset. The booklet of questions and answers in which he outlines the basic tenets of the Ageless Wisdom is a gem of succinctness and yet it covers everything we need to know for living our lives according to the Laws of Life, including reincarnation and karma (cause and effect).

The law of Brotherhood
While the teachings of the Space Brothers which Adamski gave in his book *Inside the Space Ships* are comprehensive and profound in themselves, he later elaborated on these a good deal in publications that were only available to readers who subscribed to them and are therefore hardly

... was already installed by Adamski at the Temple of Scientific Philosophy in Laguna Beach in 1938, as reported by the *Los Angeles Times* on 30 April of that year. (See page 56.)

known among the general public, and even less generally available. In the 5-part *Cosmic Science* bulletin, a series of answers to questions from supporters and readers around the world, for instance, Adamski writes: "Evolution, or the refinement of matter is a Cosmic Law. Our own planet furnishes us proof of this. (...) But always bear in mind, Earth is not unique. Divine nature expresses the same throughout the Cosmos. (...) Remember, there is only one Creator, one Supreme Intelligence; **and all life receives equally from this one Source**."[13]

"The Universal Laws are not new or unknown to Earth's people. They have been handed down for countless centuries through our philosophical teachings. But because to the average person these teachings have been cloaked in mystery and relegated to the field of the abstract, few people recognize the kernels of Truth lost amidst the mountains of chaff. We must remember, True Philosophy is nothing more than the science of living according to the purpose for which all forms were brought into being. There must be eternal growth and blending; but never divisions."[14]

Our 'purpose for being' is explained to Adamski by the Master from Venus, as follows: "We have learned that nothing, no form whatever, can be what it is without life passing through it, or supporting it. And the life we recognize is the Divine Supreme Intelligence. Never a moment passes, even in sleep, that we are not aware of this Divine Presence." And expressing the highest state of Divine Intelligence "is the true purpose of the form 'man' ... that for which he was created. (...) The people of your world (...) have begun to think that form is all there is. But the form is only a channel through which life, or intelligence, expresses."[15]

Adamski himself explains: "When [man] understands himself, his purpose for being, and his relationship to the All, he rises in consciousness to a heavenly state of naturalness wherein...he has compassion for all. This does not mean a state of blissful unconcern. On the contrary, people who have attained this understanding are actively interested in all that goes on about them."[16]

The Laws of Life apply on every planet, says Adamski. "Earthlings, because of their deep reverence for these great Teachers, have enshrined their teachings in the world religions, not comprehending they were showing us a way of life. 'Greater things than these shall ye do,' was the promise given by one Master; yet our doubts and fears have held us in such bondage, we have not approached His simplest miracle."[17]

In *Flying Saucers Farewell* Adamski says that on the higher planets in our system education begins at birth: "A newborn child is observed lovingly and carefully to learn its thought patterns and its natural interests. This does not mean it has the privilege of ruling the home, as so often occurs on Earth! From the beginning a child is taught the value and rewards of humility, consideration for others and the indescribable joy of loving and being loved."[18] In *Cosmic Science* he adds, "[P]eople on our neighboring planets are taught a science of life from infancy. Instruction in the functioning of the mind and body, and man's relationship to the Cosmos is considered to be of paramount importance. Taught the power of thought, they learn to become masters of their minds rather than slaves to them."

In educational institutes, which are frequented by

people of all ages, instruction is given in the Universal Laws of Life. These are put into practice on a daily basis, instead of people observing special services according to their particular religious traditions, as on Earth. "All great teachers have taught the law of respect, love, and brotherhood. Jesus, whose teachings are the basis of every denomination of the Christian world, gave us one commandment ... the commandment of love without judgment. Yet look at the divisions, resentments and hatred prevalent amongst the people on Earth; all of which have laid the foundation for wars and rumors of wars confronting us on every side. If the people on other planets had lived their teachings no better than Earthlings, they, too, would be experiencing the same turmoil we find around us today."[19] Adding elsewhere: "We profess belief, and many give devout lip service, while inwardly doubting the practicality of living the Universal Laws which have been handed down through the centuries from Men of Wisdom."[20]

In reply to another question Adamski repeated: "The law of brotherhood has been handed down to us through countless ages. They [the space people] live this law."[21] Earlier, in *Inside the Space Ships*, Firkon explained: "We of other worlds who have been living unrecognized amongst you can see clearly how identity with Divine origin has been lost. People of Earth have become separate entities which are no longer truly human in expression as in the beginning they were. Now they are but slaves of habit. Nonetheless, imprisoned within these habits is still the original soul that yearns for expression according to its Divine inheritance. (...) And this is why, desiring finer and greater expression, more often than men realize, something stirring within the depths of their beings leaves the habit-bound self uneasy and restless."[22]

Adamski explains where we go wrong in our relation to others and the world: "[T]hrough ignorance [man] judges and condemns that which he sees about him. Whether he realizes it or not, by his judgments he exalts himself above the Creator; thereby causing a feeling of separation between himself and the Giver of all Life. But when he casts off the fetters forged by his carnal mind, he becomes the Knower; and is then one with the Cosmic Cause of all creation. All nature works in harmony with the Supreme Intelligence which gave it birth. Man stands alone; the sole distorter of the Law."[23]

In contrast, the space people mentioned in *Inside the Space Ships* "compared their way of life to ours quite impartially. They did not criticize or pass judgment upon us; they merely analyzed the two phases of life. They pointed out the path of brotherhood we should follow, but did not condemn us for our selfish shortcomings. Rather, theirs was an attitude of compassionate understanding for a wayward, younger brother."[24]

"Living in peace with one's fellowman is but a matter of understanding and compassion. It is a Universal Law we all must learn and apply in our daily contacts with others if we are to progress."[25] The principles which form the foundation of such living are given as follows[26]:

1. To desire no more than we actually need for our daily health and comfort.
2. To look upon all people as equals, without favoritism to any.

3. To watch and control our thoughts, which requires constant alertness.[27]
4. To appreciate and give thanks to every form for service rendered.

A parable

If life is universal, and an expression of the One Consciousness, how was it possible for Earth humanity to lose sight of this reality, which is such a fundamental part of the teachings? Adamski explains this in a parable which he used to help his audience understand who we really are and which was transcribed from a recording of one of his talks.[28] This parable also illustrates Adamski's ability to explain profound principles in the simplest terms:

"We will say there is a drop of water. Everybody knows what water is. Whether that water comes out of the faucet, by rain or out of the ocean, it is *water*, made up of the same original elements. The drop of water may be a small one, or it may be a big one. If it drops on a surface, it will have a flat bottom to it, and it will have a dome-like top. So, it is personified. It is a form, an individualized form of its own. If it could speak our language it would say: 'See me? I have a flat bottom and a rounded top. I'm made up of crystal-pure liquid known as water. You can look through me, and all that.'

"Now the water may stay there for a long time and evaporate, and finally become invisible, because it came from the Invisible to be visible in liquid form. Yet that drop of water is experiencing only what is now present. But that same drop of water can also start rolling, down a little hill, and lose itself in that rolling and the struggle – by being active, by picking up all the dust, the debris and stench, and everything else that might be in its path – and finally lose its appearance as a drop of water and form a sphere of mud, so you no longer see the water.

"The mudball now becomes personified and says: 'Now look! I'm mud.' So you say to it: 'No, you are water. Water made you.' But it tells you: 'Oh no! Where do you see any water? I'm not water, I'm mud! Can't you see me? I'm made up of all this debris, all this matter. See?' Then this ball may stop and stay in place for a while. Finally, the moisture, which is the water that made it up in the first place, dries out, or evaporates, and the mudball goes back to the dust from which it came.

"The only experience it had was the experience of being created by the drop of water into a ball of mud and rolling awhile, and being made up of different minerals as it picked them up out of rolling. It never did recognize that it was the water that was the parent of the ball. It separated itself right there, when it became the ball of mud. And that is what we do.

"Now another drop of water will keep rolling, and desires to know the truth. 'I can only see myself as a ball of mud. But if I really am water, I want to find the original part of myself from which I came. I must have come from some source to be a drop of water.' So it keeps on rolling.

"That is the way we are searching for Truth. To return to the Creator, to find our real Self. So it keeps on rolling and finally gets to the seashore. The moment it gets to the seashore, and the first wave hits it, that drop of water is absorbed completely into the body of the ocean, and the mudball too. No matter how much stench and debris was part of that mudball, or how badly perverted it was, once the vast body of water – the ocean – took it in, it purified the mudball, almost instantly. Then the drop of water again lost its little dome idea which it had in the beginning, and its little ego there, which had said, 'Look and see me, a drop of water.' It lost itself in the sea, or in the ocean. Now, since it has come there, it is now as powerful as the ocean and the sea, and will live as long as that ocean will live. And anything that takes place in that ocean, from shore to shore, that drop of water will become aware of all that action within the ocean.

"So we as cosmic people – your real self is the cosmic identity – are also everywhere like that drop of water is now – everywhere simultaneously. Anything that transpires anywhere, we should be alert to it, if we permit our minds to become cosmic with it. (…) You may call the drop of water pure spirituality, and the mud pure material. Once the two united, both were equal in every respect, except you divided them, and lost yourself in the division. (…)

"Call that self-awakened awareness. You have to awaken the mind to that reality. The mind is the separator, or the wedge in there, the ego. When you finally have that mind, which is the mud, acknowledge that it is made by something better – that it has a parent behind it, and if it wasn't for that, it would not be a mudball – then drive for the Cosmic Sea. And once you touch the fringe of it, you are part of it. That individualized intelligence which was represented by the drop of water unites with the total intelligence of the sea. So whatever goes on anywhere, in any part of it, depth, height, or width, that drop partakes of it like the mind."

The oneness of life

The same idea, condensed, Adamski expressed in his course on telepathy as follows: "The personal ego, interested only in perpetuating itself, is unaware of its unity with all manifestation; and selfishly concentrates its efforts upon the personal self. But when, through understanding, we can get the ego to turn its awareness outward, it will return to its natural free state; and the real Self will recognize its oneness with the Cosmos."[29] And elsewhere he quotes the space people as saying: "Anyone who wishes to be of help to us [the Space Brothers] will have to learn, at least to a small degree, to blend their soul consciousness with the Over-Soul of the cosmos. Then they may recognize us when we meet. Many from Earth have already met us unknowingly."[30]

This blending of consciousness, of course, has been the age-old adage of the Knowers, who counselled "Man, know thyself" (the Delphic oracle) or to ask ourselves, "Who am I?" (the Indian avatar Ramana Maharshi), while the Master from Venus told Adamski that knowledge of ourselves "is the first requisite".[31]

Not allowing their minds to separate their individual consciousness from the sea of consciousness, the space people come to Earth to help us regain that sense of oneness, and thereby save ourselves. In order to do so, says Adamski, they have expressed their desire to reveal their identities to the people of Earth, but "because of our skepticism, as well as our gullibility in accepting self-aggrandizing impostors, the visitors move quietly among us, unrecognized by the Earthlings they contact daily."[32]

"Their very appearance in our skies in friendship, carries the Cosmic message of brotherhood. For were they hostile, with their superior knowledge they could have conquered the world long ago."[33] In his course on telepathy Adamski also says: "It is through our senses that we pass judgment on conditions, persons, nations; not understanding the oneness of all with Cosmic Cause. Thus, if we are to become a peaceful unit within ourselves, we must constantly guard against these wayward senses, and subdue their criticism and prejudices; for these are the greatest causes of divisions in the family of human relations. Our personal judgments divide brother against brother – nation against nation."[34] And, "[a]ccording to what I have learned from the Brothers, the space people know and live these laws of compassionate understanding for all creation. Knowing that all manifestation is an expression of the One Creator, they do not judge nor condemn. Recognizing that all are children of the Divine Father, they have not participated in wars for millions of years."[35]

According to Adamski, space people are able to do this because they "have learned that in its natural state, all life expresses as a joyous, free execution of each action. They do not consider the performance of their daily chores burdensome, but rather, view them as a privilege whereby they can render further service to Cosmic Cause by enabling it to express unhampered through them. (…)

"When we are able to employ this same joyful, relaxed state of mind in our daily living, our consciousness will be raised to the place where impressions of universal value will come to us naturally. This does not mean that man will then ignore the world around him, for he was born on this earth to live as a participating unit with the whole of humanity..."[36] In order to achieve this state, the first step must be to coordinate our reactions to a unity with, and understanding of, underlying Cause, "by utilizing the law of patience," [37] working, he says, "until you honestly feel a oneness with all creation...".[38] That, in a word, is the purpose of our lives, to overcome our sense of separation and re-establish this deep-felt connection with all life. "Impatience is a major cause of unbalance in our lives, and interferes when impressions are coming to us. Our zealous desires often inject our own sense ideas in place of waiting for the full thought... Logic tells us to be patient and observant. We should learn to obey logic from the Cosmic angle."[39]

The Venusian Master put it thus: "Since we have learned that life is all-inclusive and that we *are* that life, we know that we can hurt nothing without hurting ourselves."[40] The Master further explains that mankind must realize that the notion 'universal' includes the physical forms within it, just as everything that happens within the Universe is contained within the Divine Intelligence: "That is why we are as much concerned with your world and your life as we are with our own, for we are all in the same kingdom of the Supreme Intelligence. We have learned and lived this for all these hundreds and thousands of years. Because of this understanding we cannot injure with a motive of injuring as you do on Earth."[41]

Man, Adamski says, as one of the most vivid and

urgent illustrations of the interconnectedness of life, "must first learn to control his emotions, his sense reactions, his selfish desires; and to understand that he is one with **all creation**. He must comprehend that the atoms vibrating in his present body have been used and reused throughout creation; therefore, they have participated in every phase, from the lowest conceivable form, to immense planetary bodies that ages ago were absorbed back into space. There are no divisions except those man has imposed upon himself!"[42]

The Space Brothers, on the other hand, Adamski says, "respect and humbly study all life, knowing they can learn even from a newborn infant. They guard carefully the workings of their own minds, and are alert to the thoughts which they host; welcoming those of a Cosmic nature, and discarding those containing divisions and personality which would create misunderstanding and conflict."[43] If we are to grow, "we will have to begin taking more interest in understanding our thoughts and their effects upon us as well as others, turning our minds toward the source of these thoughts and the reasons we allow them to possess us. In reality, we should be the masters of our thoughts, yet how many of us are?"[44]

Brotherhood in practice
In his *Science of Life* study course, Adamski teaches that the mind (or personality) is nothing more than the conglomerate of our senses, and therefore limited to the world of effects, and is itself informed by consciousness, or the human soul (cause): Living in the world of three dimensions, or effects, man has "left the fourth dimension

[consciousness] to mysteries and theories. And only here and there an individual could see the relationship of all dimensions. (...) Man has learned much about the three-dimensional world and now it is time for him to blend his knowledge with the four-dimensional invisible world around him." In order to unite that which is divided in man, "the mind must be willing to be taught by consciousness. And remember, consciousness is the soul of any form which makes life possible."[45]

In describing how the Space Brothers have attained their level of relative perfection Adamski actually hints at how we may achieve the same: "They have a knowledge of the working of their bodies, of the power of thought, and a control over their minds that would be impossible for us to emulate. They have perceived their purpose for being, their relationship to the Cosmos, and the unity of all contained therein. With this understanding has come a humbleness and compassion such as we cannot conceive. For as [man] grows in the Universal ways of Life, he is able to see the cause behind all acts; and he then develops compassion for all."[46]

While the space people "live in compassionate humility at all times, both in respect to their fellowman and to their Creator"[47], humanity assumes "the planet belongs to Man, with each claiming his small plot; while our neighbors in space realize their planet belongs to the Creator. So as one large family they share its products equally."[48] Whereas on Earth "our lack of understanding of natural principles and causes, along with the greed to get all we can for our money and effort, has led us into a war with Nature. We have set up a chain reaction which, when traced, will be found to affect all life, from the lowly insect to man himself."[49]

This notion is also conveyed to Giorgio Dibitonto by Raphael (Ramu) who tells his Italian contactee: "The Earth is out of harmony, and disintegrating vibrations, like the scourges that lash her sorrowing multitudes, create ever-widening zones on the planet where the life energies are undermined."[50] And on one of Dibitonto's sojourns on a cigar-shaped spaceship a man "whose appearance evoked admiration immediately" says: "The under-developed state of many parts of the world results in starvation and death through undernourishment and disease, as a consequence of poverty. That is a heavy burden of guilt to be borne by those people who have a thriving culture."[51]

During their final meeting, as described in *Inside the Space Ships*, Orthon tells Adamski: "If man is to live without catastrophe, he must look upon his fellow being as himself, the one a reflection of the other."[52] Therefore, on other planets, "All production is for the benefit of everyone, with each receiving according to his needs. And since no medium of exchange such as money is involved, there are no 'rich'; there are no 'poor'. But all share equally, working for the common good. This may well be called a system of production for use."[53]

Referring to President Johnson's 'Great Society' legislation, Adamski wrote: "[T]o have a healthy and prosperous society, that which causes the most trouble must be removed. As we all know, this stigma is poverty in the midst of plenty. It is the cause of sickness, crime, and the many evils that we know and when it is removed these bad results will vanish."[54] This pinpoints exactly the arena where the Space Brothers tell us we should express the oneness of our spiritual nature if we are to overcome the current crises that beset the planet and which they foretold – economic, financial, social, political and ecological.

Interestingly, according to Benjamin Creme, Maitreya has said that the solution is already in our hands: "Firstly, men must see themselves as brothers, sons of the One Father... Throughout the world there are men, women and little children who have not even the essentials to stay alive; they crowd the cities of many of the poorest countries in the world... My brothers, how can you watch these people die before your eyes and call yourselves men?"[55] He counsels us: "Take your brother's need as the measure for your action and solve the problems of the world. There is no other course."[56]

Benjamin Creme has said that Maitreya is the World Teacher expected by all the major religions under different names – Maitreya Buddha, Kalki Avatar, Imam Mahdi, the Christ, et cetera, and His coming signals the collapse of our current systems which no longer serve the needs of humanity as it increasingly responds to the incoming cosmic energies of synthesis and unity that accompany this historic event and which will shape the new Age of Aquarius.

In reference to the Second Coming, Adamski asked: "What chance would Jesus have if He were to return to Earth in fulfillment of Bible Prophecy? And if He did, who would recognize Him and be sure of His identity? (...) If He healed the sick as He did before, would He not be branded a charlatan and persecuted by the medical associations of the world? If He performed miracles, would He not be accused of practicing mysticism? (...) Unless one's conscious perception is awakened, rather than sleeping under the blanket of materialism, how could one hope to recognize a man who in appearance would be no different from others? Were Jesus to return and be accepted, it would mean that all of our present systems would be overthrown to make way for His Cosmic Teachings. Are we prepared for this?"[57]

Prepared or not, this seems to be exactly what is happening today to our worn-out structures, based as they are on greed and competition. Where there is complete freedom, initiative flourishes, Adamski reassured a questioner who wondered if the lack of competition would not stifle all initiative. "The spirit of competition could easily be replaced by an individual's desire to do the best he can according to his ability."[58]

However, "under our present system, even though our inner desires may yearn toward other goals, our first consideration must be making a living to meet our daily needs. Since no man exists without these deep-seated aspirations, could the limitations now placed upon him by circumstances be alleviated, he would be able to pursue them naturally for the betterment of himself and all mankind... I have been told degrees of intellectuality on our neighboring planets are comparable to those on Earth. There are the laborers, the artists, the scientists, the farmers, and so on. All are necessary for a well-balanced civilization, so all are respected equally; because they play their essential roles in solving the problems of the planet. It is their custom to work only a few hours each week, devoting the remainder of their time to study, recreation and travel... Would such a way of life be insipid? Would it not give us the leisure to unfold our natural talents, rather than stifle them? Remember, where there is interest, you will always find incentive toward something finer. The boredom which most Earthlings fear, is the result of mental immaturity."[59]

Despite life on other planets being relatively ideal, the Space Brothers "are doing the same as we. They too are traveling the pathway of life, learning lessons every day."[60] They come to Earth to work and live because man is inherently a traveler, Adamski says. "He enjoys visiting new places, seeing new sights, and meeting new people. The fortunate ones in our world who are able to spend months or years in other countries, learning their languages, their customs, and receiving new ideas from the people with whom they come in contact, gain much knowledge in this way. (...) It is regrettable that our monetary system makes it impossible for the vast majority of Earth's people to enjoy extensive travel. Since there is no commercialism on our neighboring planets, and since (...) it is their custom for all the inhabitants to be given vacations spent in space travel as a part of their education, it is natural that some of them should choose to come to Earth for a sojourn."[61] After all, "Travel is a source of unending practical education which gives not only pleasure but lessons of lasting value, never forgotten."[62]

Saving ourselves

Adamski advocated taking responsibility for our own lives and his message was ultimately one of emancipation, endowing each individual with the power to implement the Universal Law in our own life: "We cannot expect the governments of the world to adopt a conciliatory attitude toward one another unless the peoples themselves have already done so. For as long as the masses continue their discriminations and hatreds, they are not yet ready for a more advanced way of living."[63] After all, "[e]ach individual is a radiating center of influence, whose ultimate circumference no one can accurately perceive."[64] It is necessary therefore, he says, to "[w]atch your thoughts and see if they are of the type you really desire to entertain. If not, change them to conform with your better aspirations. Become the master of your mind ... not its slave. Watch your attitude towards others – business contacts, friends, strangers, members of your own family. Are you polite to some, tolerant toward others, and argumentative with those closest to you? Or are you compassionate and kind to all alike?

"The world as a whole is composed of billions of individuals, each of whom is important as a radiating center of action. And the whole cannot be changed unless, and until, each small part is brought into cooperation and harmonious coordination with all others. In the human family we know this as the Brotherhood of Man."[65]

According to Adamski, there is every hope for humanity to save itself: "Each individual lives his own life, makes his own future destiny, and writes his own history. In the Cosmic Plan no man is ever left stranded without hope. Once the desire is awakened in a man's heart for a better understanding of himself, his purpose for being, and his relationship to the Cosmic All, the way is always opened for him to attain his goal."[66]

"All planets are class rooms in the Cosmic School of Life; and there exist many grades... Earth is one such class room in the Cosmos. It is a holy place, where we are given the opportunity to grow in understanding that we may climb to another rung on the endless Ladder of Life."[67] "What we need to concern ourselves with here, is to try to master the lessons of the present that we may the more speedily inherit the future that is surely our destiny."[68]

Earth may be compared with a kindergarten where children with many different character traits learn to work and play together, arrogant and timid, introvert and extravert, patient and impatient, kind and cruel. "It is the purpose of the kindergarten classes to teach these individuals to blend harmoniously with one another. In such a manner self-control is established and group coordination can be brought about. (...) With increased understanding comes greater appreciation, joy and accomplishments."[69]

As the Venusian teacher told Adamski: "There is nothing wrong with your Earth, nor with its people, except that in their lack of understanding they are young children in the universal life of the One Supreme Being. You have been told that in our worlds we live the Creator's laws, while as yet on Earth you only talk of them."[70] In other words, "as long as we harbor fear, hatred and greed in our hearts, we are not living our belief in God. True belief in God is a way of life."[71]

However, adds Adamski, "Due to our lack of understanding of the continuity of life, the average infant is immediately started upon a pathway of indoctrination to enforce it to conform with our accepted preconceived ideas."[72] "Understanding," he elaborates elsewhere, "is knowledge lived. When we understand the purpose behind each act, we do not judge. We then become observers, to evaluate all manifestations in relationship to Cosmic Cause, which gave them birth."[73]

"Understanding of the universal law both uplifts and restricts. As it is now with us, so it could be on your Earth," the Venusian Master told Adamski. "Lifted up by your knowledge, this same understanding would make it impossible for you to move in violence against your brothers. You would know that the same conviction, inherent in every individual being, which makes him feel that he has the divine privilege of directing his own life and shaping his own destiny, even though it be by the path of trial and error, applies equally to any group, nation or race of mankind."[74] To which Adamski added elsewhere: "Each planet, each individual, must fulfill its own destiny by solving its own problems."[75] For our planet, he says, "is not subordinate to the others in our system. ... So, since the progress which our world makes toward taking its rightful place with its sister planets lies in the hands of each individual living here, let us try to fulfill our destiny with joy in our hearts."[76]

About his own progress Adamski remarked: "To say that I have grown to the place where I live as they do would not be true. But since man is eternal, each successful effort takes me a step farther along the path of progress. It requires constant effort, with eternity in which to succeed. The wise man knows that only as he learns to live moment by moment will progress be his; for it is always the present.

The past is gone and cannot be changed regardless how one might like to change it. The future can never be reached, not even the coming moment. When it arrives, it is the present. These are the lessons Earth's inhabitants are to learn."[77]

The space people "are more advanced than we, and have reached that stage only by passing through and conquering the experiences we are now undergoing. They understand the struggles confronting Earthlings, therefore feel a deep compassion for us. As I have said many times, they have told me repeatedly that they only want to help us – if we will but listen and accept their help."[78]

If we do, says Adamski, "[w]e must learn to live humbly, respecting our fellow man regardless of his color of skin or position in life"[79], each of us, in our daily lives. "For it is the daily living that is all important! And each must do this for himself."[80]

Notes

Teachings of the Masters of Wisdom:
1 A.J. Gulyas, 'Meaningful Contact: George Adamski and the Contactees as Social Reformers'. *UFO Review* No.13, November/December 2005, p.112.
2 George Adamski (1936), *Wisdom of the Masters of the Far East*, p.58-59.
3 Ibid., p.59.
4 Ibid., p.15.
5 Ibid.
6 Ibid., p.17.
7 Ibid., p.14.
8 Ibid., p.21.

9   Ibid., pp.20-21.
10 Ibid., p.59.
11 Ibid., p.22.
12 Ibid., p.24.

The law of Brotherhood:
13 Adamski (1957-58), *Cosmic Science for the promotion of Cosmic Principles and Truth*, Part No.3, Question #56.
14 Ibid., Part No.2, Question #36.
15 Adamski (1955), *Inside the Space Ships*, pp.206-07.
16 Adamski (1957-58), Part No.2, Question #40.
17 Ibid., Part No.3, Question #44.
18 Adamski (1961), *Flying Saucers Farewell*, p.82.
19 Adamski (1957-58), Part No.5, Question #99.
20 Ibid., Part No.1, Question #10.
21 Ibid., Part No.2, Question #25.
22 Adamski (1955), pp.116-17.
23 Adamski (1958), *Telepathy: The Cosmic or Universal Language*, Part I, p.9.
24 Ibid., Part II, p.28.
25 Adamski (1957-58), Part No.2, Question #40.
26 Adamski (1961), pp.82-83.
27 According to Adamski, not even the Space Brothers manage to do this all the time. "But when they catch themselves erring, those who have not turned into the detour of egotism immediately change to the universal aspect, looking upon their error as a lesson to be remembered and not to be repeated." Ibid.

A parable:
28 Taken from Daniel Ross, 'Adamski's Cosmic Reality Is Timeless', in Hachiro Kubota (ed.), *UFO Contactee* (GAP-Japan Newsletter International Edition) No.10, February 1995, pp.5-7. [Edited transcription from the recording of a private talk which Adamski gave in April 1965.]

The oneness of life:
29 Adamski (1958), Part III, p.41.
30 Adamski [1962], 'How to Know A Spaceman If You See One', in G. Barker (ed.) (1966), *Book of Adamski*, p.53.
31 Adamski (1955), pp.201-02.
32 Adamski (1957-58), Part No.5, Question #87.
33 Ibid., Part No.3, Question #58.

34 Adamski (1958), Part I, p.21.
35 Adamski (1957-58), Part No.3, Question #54.
36 Adamski (1958), Part I, p.10.
37 Ibid., Part I, p.21.
38 Ibid., p.30.
39 Ibid., Part III, p.42.
40 Adamski (1955), p.204.
41 Ibid., p.202.
42 Adamski (1958), Part II, p.26.
43 Adamski (1957-58), Part No.4, Question #70.
44 Adamski (1961), p.81.

Brotherhood in practice:
45 Adamski (1964), *Science of Life* study course, Lesson Five: 'Consciousness, The Intelligence and Power of All Life'.
46 Adamski (1957-58), Part No.3, Question #60.
47 Ibid., Part No.4, Question #71.
48 Ibid., Part No.1, Question #9.
49 Adamski (1961), p.77.
50 Giorgio Dibitonto (1990), *Angels in Starships*, pp.20-21.
51 Ibid., p.82.
52 Adamski (1955), p.239.
53 Adamski (1957-58), Part No.1, Question #18.
54 Adamski (1965b), *Cosmic Bulletin*, December 1964, p.14.
55 Benjamin Creme (ed.) (1992), *Messages from Maitreya the Christ*, Message No.11.
56 Ibid., Message No.52.
57 Adamski (1957-58), Part No.5, Question #94.
58 Adamski (1965a), *Answers to Questions Most Frequently Asked About Our Space Visitors And Other Planets*, 1965, p.17.
59 Adamski (1957-58), Part No.3, Question #45.
60 Adamski (1961), p.80.
61 Adamski (1957-58), Part No.5, Question #96.
62 Adamski (1961), p.87.

Saving ourselves:
63 Adamski (1957-58), Part No.3, Question #44.
64 Ibid., Part No.4, Question #72.
65 Ibid.
66 Ibid., Question #80.
67 Adamski (1958), Part II, p.24.
68 Adamski (1957-58), Part No.2, Question #39.

69 Adamski (1961), p.78.
70 Adamski (1955), p.94.
71 Adamski (1957-58), Part No.1, Question #10.
72 Ibid., Part No.3, Question #52.
73 Adamski (1958), Part III, p.40.
74 Adamski, (1955), p.93.
75 Adamski (1957-58), Part No.2, Question #25.
76 Ibid., Part No.1, Question #10.
77 Adamski (1961), p.91. Cf the teaching of J. Krishnamurti about the importance of being constantly alert to the trappings of the mind in e.g. *The Future is Now* (1988).
78 Adamski (1957-58), Part No.5, Question #89.
79 Ibid., Part No.2, Question #23.
80 Ibid., Part No.1, Question #1.

PART TWO: WRITINGS

The two texts by George Adamski in Part Two help, each at their own level, to broaden our view of life.

The first is titled 'The Magnificent Perception' and was taken from Adamski's book *Cosmic Philosophy*. While parts of this book were reworked from texts which he wrote in the 1930s, this particular treatise stands apart in terms of style, 'colour' and rhythm from not only the rest of that book, but from almost everything else he has written. Ranking among the most evocative of his writings, it relates the coming into existence of matter as a result of the original

Cause sending out its creative vibration, and man's journey upward through the successive planes of existence back to his spiritual origins. It is almost impossible to read these pages and not think of the Hubble space telescope's dramatic photographs of the Carina Nebula, where new stars are said to be born. Readers may also find this text reminiscent of the story of creation in the Stanzas of Dzyan from H.P. Blavatsky's *The Secret Doctrine*.

The second text is titled 'The Space People' and is published here for the first time. Giving a comprehensive view of life on Venus and comparing it with life on Earth, this article has previously only been distributed to members of the Get Acquainted Program in December 1964.

Comparing these two texts the conclusion must be that the first was inspired, at the very least, by the exalted Being whom Adamski met on his sojourns on the motherships, as described in his book *Inside the Space Ships*.[1] Readers will find several similarities with the teachings which Adamski was given by the Masters with Whom he studied in Tibet. While certainly more mundane – if that term can apply to extraterrestrial life – the second text is no less interesting in its detailed description of life on Venus, one of the most advanced planets in our system according to the Ageless Wisdom teaching.

These texts are reproduced here with kind permission from the George Adamski Foundation.

---

[1] See also Benjamin Creme (2010), *The Gathering of the Forces of Light – UFOs and Their Spiritual Mission*, p.55.

The Magnificent Perception
by George Adamski

*(Taken from **Cosmic Philosophy**, 1961. Reproduced with kind permission from G.A.F. International/George Adamski Foundation of Vista, California, USA.)*

Prelude

The roll of the tides and the waves and the rising and setting of suns, the whirling of atoms and worlds are all tuned to the Cosmic Plan yet are subject to time and space.

Time is the instrument used to measure the movement of Being – the element action creates in its path from the formless to the formed. In Eternity always you are, but in time you're unstable, inconstant.

Sit here at the center of all and look out on your flux of expression. As the moon to the vision of man passes through all the various phases yet remains still an orb complete without change or point of division, so you through your phases shall pass; moral eyes shall see change and division yet you are a circle complete – you are endless, eternal, abiding.

Look forth from these eternal heights, from the heart of your unified being; look down towards the plains of desire where your destiny finds its fulfillment. Look closely and firmly perceive that the break which you one time envisioned is nothing more than mortal illusion; that there is but the unified whole.

Always you are One, you are All, as a centralized

point of Being. Undying, unchanging – the Consciousness, Cause, and the Action – evolving, transmuting a form to a unified state of awareness.

From action to action you pass like a great shuttle weaving new patterns – on the loom of Eternity weaving a pattern of beauty called Life. The fine silver thread which you use is Cosmic Consciousness, binding together each stitch in true lines of perfection; creating in patient evolvement the unified Love Mantle of All. Each thought and each conscious emotion weaves the Pattern of exact direction, in time uniting the parts and the Allness, absorbing the All in the One.

The Word

In the beginning there was but the Word: no mortal mind can know the Word in full for it contains all knowledge and all Power, and only that which is Itself the Word can know or understand potentially. But through a mighty action the Word was imaged into primal form; in form so fine that only Cause could know its attributes or view its being. It incarnated through the whole of substance and impregnated all matter with Its presence till the place of a tremendous void there grew the second or the form-creation.

Virgin was this creation in the image of the Word, and filled with all the power of pure wholeness, for it was but one great united form, the body of Cosmic Cause whom we in reverence have called "The Word."

Through all space the Word reverberated; It set in motion all the Primal Essence until the whole span of Infinity swayed to the Heart-beat of the Mighty Oneness.

Rhythm on rhythm rose and fell in one great undivided harmony, for deep within the bosom of the Word there surged the wondrous Love Song of Creation.

Greater and greater the Heart of Space was stirred until at last the Song was breathed into a living thing. Each motion as an elemental tone within the mighty symphony and every tiny particle of substance was tuned into accord with every other unit in all space. And thus the impulse of Cosmic Will became a law that ne'er can broken be within the scope of everlasting action. (This Law involves the principle of true affinity.)

Were it possible for any of the Cosmic vibrations to unite contrary to this Primary Law and cause a discord in the mighty paeon their span of such expression would be contained within one moment's quivering vibration, for discord cannot last within the Whole whose very fact of being rests upon the immutable law of harmony. There is no loss of equilibrium within the scope of Cosmic Rhythm that shall not be again absorbed and reunited into Wholeness. For nothing can break the Melody that has forever throbbed within the Heart of That which is, Itself, Infinity.

Creation as a whole makes up the song that rises and falls in its impassioned cadence, expressing in the glory of calm Silence all that the Word has been, is, and shall be; voicing with soundless sounds and formless beauty the pulsing force that blends and inter-blends into new rhythms. The Breath of the All-Creative Intelligence is sent forth in peaceful, silent tones of consciousness and in the womb of illimitable space each new creating stirs with quickened life and becomes another true note in the endless Song of Action.

Out of Cosmic Cause are worlds and planets whirled into existence; out of such formless beauty has evolved form upon form until at last there came one form so perfect in its geometric pattern that it possessed the possibilities of understanding Cause. And so into this form was poured the Breath which speaks the rhythm of creation into being, and it was given power to perceive all existence; and it was also blessed with power to name that which before had been but nameless.

And this creation, highest of them all, was known as Man, born out of That which has no ending; given dominion, consciousness and love and power over all the lesser things. But he descended into depths of sleep, became unconscious of the vaster kingdoms, forgetful of the Glory that exists and dreamed, instead, into existence the changing image of mortality.

Oh, Son of God and Son of Man, lift up all things within your sight; let your heart make known that which the sight doth not reveal and from the womb of Cosmic Cause which is the source of all creation awaken into the birth of a Magnificent Perception. Awaken into the realm of true Being. Let the strong fingers of your will draw you again into full consciousness. Rise from your earthly couch of slumber and perceive the beauty of your present Existence.

This planet earth that we call our home was brought into its present state of being through that cosmic law of affinity, the great magnetic principle of attraction, and all that therein grows and multiplies is of the one and only Cosmic Power.

Each form that with our mortal eyes we view is but

a point in action in the whole – a minute bit of elemental substance moving to ever changing patterns and designs; impelled and impregnated with all-abiding consciousness. There is no tiniest unit in the Whole that does not bend an ear to the Law which Fathers it and causes it to be. And all that we perceive with mortal eyes and know with our consciousness is but the effective image of the Cause Intelligence, which formless is, yet causes forms to be; which knows no limitations and no bond yet creates transient dense conditions that move and change within the bosom of incomprehensible Eternity.

And every unit in the whole of Being, each atom and each spark of consciousness reveals without a mark of limitation, if we but seek its heart, the perfect image of Infinity. And each of the little passing points of action which we in earthly terms have labelled time, speak within the moment of their being the fullness of Eternity. Just as the drop of water from the ocean reveals the character of that from which it came; and every sunbeam traveling through space reflects the composition of the sun and reverberates[1] the image of that orb in all of the glory of its full expression.

We as children of the Cosmos, are in the process of reflecting the understanding of our Source. All action is the echo of the Word as It passes through the vast arcades of space, and in Its passing creates time and form.

We must open our eyes of consciousness and view in all Its magnitude and beauty, the living, breathing image of the Word.

---

1 The original text has the non-existent "revibrates" here.

The Name

The Word is changeless, whole and complete. The Name personifies the Word – divides Its vastness into many parts, gives place and form to each and every part and power of utterance in an auditory state. The whirling mass of substance called the Earth is to the mortal ears a mighty name, for on its surface humankind evolves and learns a tongue with which to speak the Name of That which in Itself is nameless, yet Earth shall change and pass away in Time, to reunite within the Cosmos. The Word has always been, will always be, the Name has a beginning and an ending.

The Word has never given forth a Name and never shall, for in such act would lose its endless and eternal state of Being. But Man, to whom free-will and power was given, who slumbers deep and dreams his mortal dreams, has in his waking moments labelled action and given name to consciousness and form. His eyes at first were dim with mortal slumber; he saw but vaguely through the mist of sleep, and only felt the coarsest of frequencies that shaped the holy substance into form, but those he named so he might build a memory of parts to guide his future waking states, for only by such means can he evolve to recognition of Cosmic Allness.

Little by little man's awareness of that which he encounters expands, and clearer grows his vision till at last his conscious awareness beholds the transcendent Cause behind the Name.

Out of the Primal Essence has come forth, charged with the Power of the Word, the manifested utterance of Cause. The planets, worlds, the moon, the stars and suns, the leafing trees, the song bird and the rain, the beasts, the crawling reptiles and the dew, each in its own tongue, expresses the Word. But man has given unto each a Name and it is there that his attention lies. Manifestation has become his God and he has placed the Name above the Word, which nameless is and silent and unseen yet causes all the named things to be.

Relativity

Matter manifests as an effect of the Cause impulse that rises from the Word. As a pebble dropped in the center of a still pool will send an impulse through the whole clear mass and stir its farthest boundaries into motion, so was the Primal Substance caused to vibrate by the Cosmic Impulse. And as the nearest wavelets are finer than those at the ultimate extreme so is the substance close to the heart of Creation finer than that upon the outer edge. Each impulse of the Word that has manifested into the realms of matter has evolved into its formed state of being through a primal motion or centralized impulse, out of which grew a heavier motion, swelling into greater perceptibility. The primal frequency goes into expansion without the smallest loss of energy.

We know that in the pool of clearest water the first wave that was started, in its passing, gave to the next its force and animation. And that, in turn, imparted added motion unto the following molecules of water. Without the unity of the whole mass no particle could know the primal action. The cosmos is like unto the pool from out whose center flows the rhythmic motion – it is the clear calm sea of undivided consciousness upon whose surface there arises innumerable wavelets of vibration. Each form, in turn, contains the same – beginning with one basic impulse evolving to countless particles of motion, each one attuned unto primal urge. Again, each tiny central point of action is offspring of the Great Heart of motion. To the understanding of the mortal man these countless points of action are perceived as separate entities within the varied kingdoms. Upon the earth man gives the name of mineral unto the denser substance that he sees; a little higher is the vegetable, and then there comes the animal and fowl, which leads up to the consciousness of man who separates the Allness into parts and draws a line where no such line could be, for through the whole vastness of the Cosmos the Primal Impulse incarnates itself and as the ripple in the pool gave up itself to create something greater, so does each manifested form of each kingdom release itself into evolvement. The innumerable minerals give up their impulse to plant life, the plant, in turn, releases energy unto the higher consciousness of flesh. There is nothing that can live alone, nor any spark of energy destroyed. All impulse lives and acts eternally, passing from form to form and in its passing charges all substance with emotion and creates ripples on the Sea of Being.

Substance is in the process of evolvement; consciousness, in the process of expression. Up and down the vast scale the force moves rapidly into expression, touching one particle of matter, then another – blending the two or more into a chord of harmony, just as the fingers of a man pluck music from the mute strings of his harp. To produce a perfect melody the strings must be set in motion many, many times, making new tonal combinations – now soft and low, now rising to crescendo; one time in rapturous swinging rhythm, then changing to a lingering minor key – all strings awaiting the touch that stirs them into life within the melody. Each string is vital to the total Song.

So it is with the Song of Creation – each atom of substance is used eternally, now making up a rose bush or a tree; now mingling within man, now in the beast; descending into form and then once more ascending to invisibility; expressing through fire, water, earth and air, and ether finer than man can know; from the coarse pulsation that produces stone to a motion higher than the speed of light; from radiation down into vibration and back again the Primal Essence moves. From the formless into the densest matter and back again into the higher state, each atom relative unto all others, cooperating and exchanging places. Within the Cosmos there is no destruction but only newness by a ceaseless action; all substance changing and transmuting but never for an instant's time withholding. In an endless array of patterns and designs from formless into formed in unfolding the wondrous picture of eternity.

There is no greater law than that of conscious action, for upon it rests continuous Creation. Energy acting upon itself gives birth to time and space, the relative elements of the Cosmos that cause conception of the state called form. Each thing depends in part upon another and may be traced back to a common source.

Permission granted by copyright holders, 2010. © Copyright G.A.F. International/George Adamski Foundation, Vista, California, USA.

THE SPACE PEOPLE.   Copyright by
━━━━━━━━━━━━━━━━━━━━━━   J. Adamski
by George ADAMSKI

As my meetings have been mostly with the people from VENUS, I will give a
few comparisons of their human relations and behavior, with our own.

They have made a detailed study of nature and find the Cosmic Father impregnating the material elements of the Mother-Planet, and supplying each form with the Cosmic Breath, that it may grow and serve all other parts of creation. They have so sensitized themselves that they can feel the pulse of the blade of grass, and the breath of the rock. To them all human beings are a manifestation of the Cosmic Breath, lending life and energy to each individualised form.

As they studied the trees, flowers, rocks, the birds and animals, and observed how each was fulfilling the purpose for which it was created, they came to the conclusion that Nature is God's Own Law in action.
So Nature could be called a mother of the Supreme Intelligence, because it is through this mother that the Supreme Intelligence expresses. Just as the mother's body supplies all the material needed for the little form that is being built within her own, so Mother Nature supplies the needs of all of the forms that are born from her body.

By these observations they have come closer to knowing the Father and His purpose than we of Earth have.

BIRTH: Their children are conceived, nurtured and honored, with this always in mind: They know that each individualized form, for which they have been priviledged to provide a body, has had endless experiences. They honor the dweller in the temple of the body as an expression of Divine Principle. Conception takes place in a womb of love and there are no sex relations during the gestation period. On Earth this reverence is not given and relationship continues, thus causing many crippled conditions.

INFANCY : When an infant is very young it's mind has not received too many impressions from its present surroundings, and there are pictures and feelings that radiate from the Inner Spark of Life within the form. The Builder of the form, the All Inclusive Intelligence, is in free state. Parents on Venus know this and have learned much from their children.

INCARNATION One child may be from Saturn and has incarnated on Venus to learn a certain phase of life that has not been expressed, and also to serve in forming balance of planetary knowledge. This has always been the case; there are those on Earth, that have had experiences on all of the planets of our system, and each one contributes to the progress of the Earth, intellectually, culturally and scientifically.

The blessing is that inhabitants of Venus never try to force their own will upon a child, nor in any way try to have them mold their lives according to their own pattern. They know that each individual has its own destiny. They will guide and care for a child, but never interfere with its individuality. Should anything happen to the parents the children are cared for by the community, for all phases of their society are as closely knit together as their family units. And the child would not feel a loss or separation from his parents.

I believe that you can see, with this attitude towards themselves and others, just what their homelife is like. They have their chores as we have, but most of their work is done by machines designed for that purpose.
As an example: They have an attractor that gathers all particles of dust from their homes; the dust is not released outside but is deposited in containers provided for that purpose. The dust is gathered from these containers and taken to a central plant, where it is processed to extract the minerals from the particles, for they do not waste anything.

First page of George Adamski's manuscript for his article 'The Space People' (1964).

The Space People
by George Adamski

(Distributed to members of GAP in 1964. Published here for the first time, with kind permission from G.A.F. International/ George Adamski Foundation of Vista, California, USA.)

As my meetings have been mostly with the people from *VENUS*, I will give a few comparisons of their human relations and behavior with our own.

They have made a detailed study of nature and find the Cosmic Father impregnating the material elements of the Mother-Planet, and supplying each form with the Cosmic Breath, that it may grow and serve all other parts of creation. They have so sensitized themselves that they can feel the pulse of the blade of grass, and the breath of the rock. To them all human beings are a manifestation of the Cosmic Breath, lending life and energy to each individualized form.

As they studied the trees, flowers, rocks, the birds and animals, and observed how each was fulfilling the purpose for which it was created, they came to the conclusion that Nature is God's Own Law in action.

So Nature could be called a mother of the Supreme Intelligence, because it is through this mother that the Supreme Intelligence expresses. Just as the mother's body supplies all the material needed for the little form that is being built within her own, so Mother Nature supplies the needs of all the forms that are born from her body.

By these observations they have come closer to

knowing the Father and His purpose than we of Earth have.

Birth: Their children are conceived, nurtured and honored, with this always in mind: They know that each individualized form, *for which they have been privileged to provide a body*, has had endless experiences. They honor the dweller in the temple of the body as an expression of Divine Principle. *Conception takes place in a womb of love and there are no sex relations during the gestation period.* On Earth this reverence is not given and relationship continues, thus causing many crippled conditions.

Infancy: When an infant is very young its mind has not received too many impressions from its present surroundings, and there are pictures and feelings that radiate from the Inner Spark of Life within the form. The Builder of the form, the All-Inclusive Intelligence, is in [a][1] free state. Parents on Venus know this and have learned much from their children.

Incarnation: One child may be from Saturn and has incarnated on Venus to learn a certain phase of life that has not been expressed, and also to serve in forming balance of planetary knowledge. This has always been the case; *there are those on Earth, that have had experiences on all of the planets of our system, and each one contributes to the progress of the Earth, intellectually, culturally and scientifically.*

---

[1] Apparently missing words have been added in square brackets. Obvious typing errors have been corrected without indication. In addition, some notes have been added by the current author to alert readers to correspondences with other sources. Spelling has been made consistent for US English.

The blessing is that inhabitants of Venus never try to force their own will upon a child, nor in any way try to have them mold their lives according to their own pattern. They know that each individual has its own destiny. They will guide and care for a child, but never interfere with its individuality. Should anything happen to the parents the children are cared for by the community, for all phases of their society are as closely knit together as their family units. And the child would not feel a loss or separation from his parents.

I believe that you can see, with this attitude towards themselves and others, just what their home life is like. They have their chores as we have, but most of their work is done by machines designed for that purpose. As an example, They have an attractor that gathers all particles of dust from their homes; the dust is not released outside but is deposited in containers for that purpose. The dust is gathered from these containers and taken to a central plant, where it is processed to extract the minerals from the particles, *for they do not waste anything*.

Our space friends have tried to awaken us to the reality of our own misguided thinking; they can understand us, for they too have had to discipline their minds, and divert the individual ego into channels of service for others. They are interested in accomplishment, not for themselves, but for the betterment of all. They are a happy people; it is not an emotional happiness, but an inner joy that comes from a task well done. They have utmost respect for everything and everyone. The man who prepares the ground for the foundation of a beautiful building, is held in as high esteem as the artist who paints the murals upon the walls. They know that each part is interdependent upon all other parts.

Honor: We in our world honor the man we feel to be brilliant, and look with disdain upon the common ditch-digger. The Venusians' whole approach to everything that they do is different from ours. If they are painting a picture or molding a statue, they have great respect for each material that they are working with, feeling that it is a living thing, and *they imbue all of their creations with a portion of their own life force*. Their statues seem alive and ready to speak. Their reactions are never of egotistical satisfaction, for they feel that they were only an instrument, through which a beautiful creation was made manifest.

I believe that it is easy for us to understand why the inhabitants of Venus, living as they do in constant awareness of, and in contact with Cosmic energy, *do not age or have diseased bodies and minds*. They do not need doctors, for everyone is familiar with the structure and operation of the body, and should there be an accident causing a broken bone, anyone could adjust the injury. They look upon the body as a garment made from the materials of the mother-planet, and loaned to the individualized expression of intelligence of each form, for a sufficient length of time for it to render certain services, and gain knowledge and wisdom from the contacts and experiences that it will have.

The garment that we call the "body" can be cared for

and maintains its usefulness and beauty for a long time; but there are advantages in having a new garment. When a new body is assembled, the cell structure, or chemical elements that go into the form, have had experiences of their own, and the *memory is held in the atom of each cell*[2]; thereby the dweller in the house can partake of the experiences of his structure. (I have explained this in my course *TELEPATHY, the Cosmic or Universal Language.*)

Death: The inhabitants of other planets know this, and they gladly discard an old garment for a new one, when the time is right. Therefore, death as we call it, is not dreaded by them, for they know that the Universe is in a state of constant change. They know that when they move on to another planet, they will be provided a body made from the elements of the planet, and that it will be much more adjustable to the conditions that they find there. It is like moving from an old house into a new one, for they find that the chemicals of the old body have served their purpose and will go into a resting period of chemical changes, that they may be used again.

History: The Venusians have in their *Libraries of Recorded History* the records of each planet in our system, the

---

2 This statement is strongly reminiscent of the esoteric notion of the three permanent atoms in the teachings of the Master D.K. through Alice A. Bailey. The permanent atoms store the vibratory rate achieved through the life experiences of the individual and form the basis for the three bodies of expression of the personality – physical, emotional and mental – in his next incarnation. See for instance Alice A. Bailey (1925), *A Treatise on Cosmic Fire*, Lucis Press, London.

structural composition of the planet, the rise and fall of the civilizations of the planet, the mechanical, scientific and cultural development of the inhabitants of the different planets.

They have told me that documents have been recorded upon our own planet Earth, that contained vast storehouses of knowledge, but that these records have been either destroyed, hidden or the original meanings completely lost through the many translations from symbol to language, and from language to language. The original manuscripts that should have been compiled, gave [a] simple, understandable explanation [of] *Creation, Evolution and Change of planets and systems*, and *the true meaning of the Garden of Eden, in reference to man living as a unit with his Cosmic Father*; descriptive examples of what takes place when man separates himself from Cosmic Cause by exaggerating his own egotistical importance, thus causing his own fall and the eventual destruction of that era of civilization; [and] the meaning of the ever forgiving Father, or Cosmic Intelligence, as depicted in the story of the Prodigal Son's Return, when he was reinstated to his original birthright, by becoming aware of his unity with Cosmic Intelligence.

These records are in our Holy Bible, but their true interpretations have been lost. I wish that I might be able to draw a more graphic picture of just what has happened in the minds of man down through the ages, as he became more and more greedy, and changed the original records to suit his own purposes, in order to keep the masses under the dominance of his own exaggerated egotistical importance; but perhaps this is not necessary, for we can see the results of this selfishness, expressing itself on all sides today.

The Space People know that the results of this type of thinking and practice lead to ultimate destruction, and they would point out to us the folly of our ways. They have told me that this has happened many times before, that every civilization that has gone down, has been warned and given an opportunity to break through their shell of limiting importance, and enjoy the privileges of the System rather than just those of one planet.

Development: The citizens of Venus are not free from making mistakes, for as I have stated, their mental development, on a scale of 100 per cent development of the capacity of the mind, *is about 20 per cent*, therefore they are bound to make mistakes. We make many mistakes and *continue to repeat them*, time after time, but when they make one, *they recognize it as such and do not repeat it*, but learn by each mistake that they make. They share their experiences with each other, and never condemn the actions of another.

Spiritual life of the Space People: Many have asked me if the people on other planets worship God as we do, and if they have places of worship, such as churches. I think that it has been well explained that they live, move and have their being in the constant awareness of the Divine Intelligence, expressing even in the blade of grass.

On one of my visits to a mother ship I was shown a moving picture on a screen, similar to our TV, of one of their buildings. There were wide steps leading to the entrance way, and [at] the end of a long room, similar to the nave in some of our beautiful old Cathedrals, covering a large wall, was "AGELESS LIFE". (This I described in *Inside the Space Ships*.)

It was breath-taking *for it was vibrant with life*. I do not believe that anyone could ever get any closer to God, than when standing in the warm embrace of this glorious portrait of Cosmic Life. And within this building were studied the wonders of the Universe and the perfect co-ordination of Cosmic Action, prompted by Cosmic Intelligence. No, we have a long way to go, before we even understand the meaning of the word *"worship"*.

Since gold is used so abundantly on Venus, I sometimes wonder if the Prophets of old did not at some time visit Venus, when they described the Gates of Heaven that were made of gold, and the streets paved with gold. Or perhaps some were from there[3] and used the word "Heaven" to depict their way of life in comparison to ours of Earth.

Homes and Public Buildings on Venus: The structural and size differences of houses are as varied on Venus as they are on Earth. For the people have individual needs and preferences in taste, for the type of building and furnishings, as we have. Their occupation determines the locale in which they live, just as it does with us.

Innately they have a very deep appreciation, almost

---

3 See also Giorgio Dibitonto (1990), *Angels in Starships*. Benjamin Creme's Master has confirmed that the angels of some of the Bible stories were, in fact, Space Brothers (see Benjamin Creme (2010), *The Gathering of the Forces of Light – UFOs and Their Spiritual Mission*, p.56).

a reverence, for beauty, and this is reflected in *their bodies, their clothing*, the furnishing of their homes, and in the structure of their buildings. They have materials with which to work that are so vibrant with soft beautiful colors that they seem alive. Since they are gentle-mannered people, *violent contrasts and extremes of design would not have a place in their pattern of harmonious living.*

The natural, abundant growth of flowers, flowering trees, shrubs and vines, and the lush foliage and grasses, are a source of never-ending inspiration for beauty of color and design.

When I was on a trip on a river in the tropics of Mexico, I was reminded of the descriptions my friends had given me of the lush, natural beauty of their planet. *There is a great deal of moisture on Venus* and little assistance is needed to have beautiful landscapes. Lovely pools and graceful statues, and grass-covered parks and terraces abound for all to enjoy.

The architecture and structural material of the community buildings also vary in color, ornamentation and size.

As there is a vast amount of *gold* on their planet, and as they do not place a *monetary value* on it, it is freely but skillfully used in decorative designs on their buildings. Perfectly executed friezes of figures and symbols in gold are used on the exterior to designate the functional use of buildings. *Slabs of cut stone* are used quite extensively as a building material. *Rock crystal*, found in strata formation, can be removed in large pieces, and is ideal for translucent, but *not transparent* wall construction. They have found a method of easy faceting, that enables them to *jewel-cut large colored rocks*. When these are used in building construction, they *look like semi-precious stones*, and some are highly polished and reflect lights in all directions.

Food preparation, etc.: We have been told by some diet experts that man is what he eats; but I would rather say, *man is what he thinks*. The chemical reactions of the food that we take into our bodies does affect the way that we feel. This is an individual thing and cannot be prescribed, en masse, for all alike. But our *emotional status* at the time the food is eaten, is an important factor in the assimilation of the elements and transformation into energy.

Some of the Space People that I have met have explained in detail their attitude towards food. They have made an extensive study of chemicals and their reactions under certain conditions, and also of the cell structure of the human body, and the fuel that is needed for the continuous replacement of cells that are ever changing.

Again, they are more fortunate than we of Earth, for the planet Venus is in *a virgin state of productivity*, with natural moistures and mineral content of the soil that vitalizes the food that they grow. Their understanding of how nature replenishes all that is needed, guides them working with natural conditions, and they *never force production*, and thus take the life-giving sustenance from the soil.

Some of their foods are cooked and some are eaten raw, but they have a method of cooking that does NOT destroy the life-germ of the elements of food. They *do eat a sufficient amount of meat* to replenish the carbon necessary for the proper functioning of the body.[4] (Since writing *Inside The Space Ships* I have learned more about their eating habits, for one of their chemists explained the importance of taking different types of foods into the body, to supply all of its parts.)

Language: On my first meeting with Orthon, as described in *Flying Saucers Have Landed*, and on several occasions when I have been on a mother ship that carried large excursions of people, I have heard them converse in their native language. *It was high-pitched and very musical*; to best describe it I would say it was like the *clear, pure tones of the flute*, not plaintive but exhilarating.

Even their spoken word carries the feeling of all-life expressing in sound, for they seem to have captured the song of the birds, the sound of the wind through the trees, and the melodious ripple of the water.

But to them the spoken word is not necessary to convey their thoughts and feeling to each other, for they have such a close unit of one with the other, that they sense the thoughts and feelings of each other. In order to have the spoken words there must be a thought, or picture of that thought in the mind. By their unity with feeling, they are in the same frequency with the thought, and it does not have to be given an audible sound for

---

[4] "By preference they are vegetarians, but not strictly so. Although they do eat meat on occasions, they do not raise cattle for slaughter." (*Cosmic Science*, Part No.1, Question #11). And, "...in view of present conditions on Earth [they] find they are healthier if they eat meat approximately once or twice a week while here." (Ibid, Part No.3, Question #43)

them to understand what is meant, for they see the picture that is in the mind.

When I first met them, I did not have to introduce myself by saying: "I am George Adamski": they knew who I was, my purpose for being on this planet, and my willingness to aid them to the best of my understanding, in serving the people of Earth. *They knew that I would have to have certain experiences in order to verify my own beliefs* or inner feelings, that I might tell others of a broader concept of the universe, and the purpose of life. So these experiences were granted to me, *not that I might be recognized as one of authority*, but that I might be a better servant to humanity.

It is unfortunate that we have so many different languages on our planet, for in translations much of the original meanings and feelings are lost, and misunderstandings arise. When each individual is able to understand and use Telepathy, as the Space People do, this difficulty will vanish, for then the true identity of the thought will be known.

Life in its true essence of expressing is so easily understood, but we have complicated our concepts of placing labels, giving names, and placing into separate compartments *that which cannot be divided*. Until we can return to the awareness that all parts of the Cosmos are interrelated, and interdependent upon all other parts, and cannot function independently, we will flounder in the confusion of effects, and not understand the Cause, or the Blueprint, or Pattern of all action.

Recreation, Games, etc.: You may ask, are the people of

Venus always of a serious mood, and think only of expressing the divinity of their being? To the second part of this question I could answer "yes", for to them the Cosmic Intelligence is always in a free state, and expresses the joy of unhampered action. *But they are not "serious" as we understand the word.*

Dance: Their music is a recording of the frequencies of the particles of the Cosmos, acting and reacting in perfect harmony, one with the other, to create a symphony of joyous expression. And when they dance, they are aware that the cells of their body are released in the free state of continuous rejuvenation that make them ever youthful. Therefore dancing is regarded by them as a form of worship or thanksgiving to Cosmic Energy, for granting them the privilege of expressing Everlasting Life. This is done by uniting every movement of their body with the rhythm of the music. Many of the native Islanders and so-called "uncivilized" tribes of this planet still carry the memory of the original purposes of the dances that they enact. But in most cases they cannot, or will not, reveal the secrets of Creation that they portray. As long as we express in our daily actions the feelings of our own personal opinions, irrespective of the feelings of others, we must remain in the field of limited energy and understanding.

The Space People enjoy all types of games, the same as we do, and many sports and competitive athletic tournaments.[5] Also cards and other types of games that

---

5 "They participate extensively in sports and games for the pure joy of playing. They enter into these with a wholehearted enthusiasm to perfect their skill and for the fun of winning." (*Cosmic Science*, Part No.3,

they play while cruising in space.

Government: As I have stated in my two books, the other planets of our system have a planetary type of government, with councillors who coordinate all problems that may arise, and take care of the needs of the different sections of their planet. They do not need laws such as we have, for their individual code of ethics is so high, that should they transgress the natural, or Universal law, they know it and make the necessary amends to right the wrong they have done.[6] There are young Councillors and older advisory Councillors, and there are those who travel space, and keep well informed on what is transpiring on the other planets and the needs of the system. By this interchange of information, they are continuously learning more about the Universe.

Planetary Changes: By the interchange they are aware of the natural changes that are taking place on the different planets of the system. They know that the planet Earth is due for a change, or shift of polarity, but they do not know just when it will be, and if partial or a complete shift.

They are interested in observing the changes that are

Question #45). "They enjoy many sports, not for competition but for development of the body." (*Answers to Questions Most Frequently Asked About Our Space Visitors and Other Planets*, p.8).

6 "For with full recognition and adequate recompense for work well done, temptations that a monetary system such as ours presents are completely eliminated." (*Cosmic Science*, Part No.1, Question #19.)

taking place on the planet; and if there should be a complete shift, they will aid in whatever way they can.[7] I have been saying for several years, *that there are large numbers of their people living among us*, and I have been asked hundreds of times: What are they doing here? One of the reasons is, that many of them *are in constant communication with their home planet*, and are alert to the changes our Earth is going through.

Space craft from *Mars* and *Venus*, and some from *Saturn* and *Jupiter* are keeping a constant vigil in our skies, recording on their instruments the changes of the magnetic lines of force in our atmosphere, and from within the body of our planet. On their home planet they have graphs that have been made when similar changes have taken place *on other planets*. By comparing their findings with these charts they are able to ascertain just what is transpiring within the body of the Earth. Our scientists have been alerted to the change through IGY[8] 1957/58 observations and have found it necessary to extend their research, for the changes were so rapid, that

---

[7] Since the time this was written, the Space Brothers "from Mars and Venus but also from Jupiter, Mercury and a few other planets, have put around our planet a ring of light which keeps it on its axis. It is very slightly off its axis, but this ring allows it, within karmic limits, to be held so that the poles do not flip..." (Benjamin Creme (2001), *The Great Approach*, p.130).

[8] IGY: International Geophysical Year. This was a major international scientific project, encompassing seven earth sciences, that lasted from 1 July 1957 to 31 December 1958. It was unique in that the USA and the Soviet Union cooperated in it, both launching satellites for the project, at a time when scientific interchange was seriously disrupted because of the Cold War.

before they could compare and record their findings, the conditions had already changed.

The coming of our neighbors from other planets is not just for the entertainment of Earthlings, nor for starting a new religion, for they are not Gods – any more than our scientists, who have been sent to strange out-of-the-way places to make observations for the IGY, were sent there to save the inhabitants. But our neighbors are willing to share their knowledge with us, if we are willing to do our part. They know that our viewpoint of life is based on false premises, and our present attitude and behavior will lead to self-annihilation. Their program is vast in scope, and the pattern well laid out. They do not judge us for our disbelief, for they know that in time all of this dilemma of fantasy will die of its own reality. And people of Earth will use their minds to think clearly and realistically, and mystery will be replaced by understanding of natural law.

Permission granted by copyright holders, 2010. © Copyright G.A.F. International/George Adamski Foundation, Vista, California, USA.

Epilogue

At a time when we had yet to come to grips with the notion of being one human family who depend for our survival on the planetary home that we all share, George Adamski saw and photographed saucer-shaped scout craft, cigar-shaped mother ships, travelled aboard both, meeting and speaking with the people from the planets from which these ships originated, and conveyed their admonitions and teachings for us, the inhabitants of Earth whose limited understanding of life imperiled our very existence.

Once he had started to inform the world of what he

learned, he became the target of 'experts' who did not share his experiences, of agents for the brokers of financial and military power whose sole purpose was to serve their own limited self-interests, and of every other would-be 'contactee' or 'expert' who thought it would make their own claims look better if they had something, anything, to say about George Adamski.

What people say and think about a man is usually informed by the breadth of their vision and the way they experience the world. If we take the facts about George Adamski, his life, and his work, and see these in the wider context of the evolution of consciousness that is made possible through the physical forms as they have evolved over time, most of the perceived controversies surrounding Adamski's claims begin to dissolve.

And if we look at the human kingdom as merely one of the forms through which the One Life expresses itself – albeit a pivotal form in a planetary sense, Adamski's teachings can be the more readily seen as practical guidelines towards building the social, economic and environmental structures and relations that reflect the fact of the one humanity. But, as Maitreya, the World Teacher, says, "Nothing happens by itself. Man must act and implement his will."[1] Knowing what we know now, therefore, we could do worse than to heed Adamski's answer to the question, in his very first book of teachings: Of what use is knowledge?

"Knowledge is useless until it is combined with action."[2]

---

1 Benjamin Creme (ed.) (1992), *Messages from Maitreya the Christ*, Message No.31.
2 George Adamski (1936), *Wisdom of the Masters of the Far East*, p.33.

APPENDIX

George Adamski publications

This overview was compiled from various sources, including the SkepticReport UFO Bibliography[1]; J. Gordon Melton and George M. Eberhart, 'The Flying Saucer Contactee Movement, 1950-1994: A Bibliography' (Chapter 10 in James R. Lewis (ed.), *The Gods Have Landed. New Religions From Other Worlds*, SUNY Press, 1995) and Paradigm Research Group[2], with corrections and additions based on the author's own research.

Books

Cosmic Philosophy
   San Diego, California, USA : G. Adamski, 1961. (iv, 87 p.)
   Freeman, South Dakota, USA : Pine Hill Press, 1972

Flying Saucers Farewell
   New York, USA; London, UK : Abelard-Schuman, 1961. (190 p.)
   Re-published as: *[The Strange People, Powers, Events] Behind the Flying Saucer Mystery*
   New York, USA : Warner Paperback Library, 1967, 1974 (159 p.)

Flying Saucers Have Landed [with Desmond Leslie]
   New York, USA : The British Book Centre, 1953, 1954, 1955, 1956, 1967, 1972 (232 p.)
   London, UK : T. Werner Laurie, 1953, 1954, 1959 (232 p.)
   London, UK : Panther Books, 1957
   New York, USA : Warner Paperback Library, 1967
   London, UK : Tiptree Book Service, 1970 (264 p.)
   London, UK : Book Club Associates, 1973
Re-published as: *Flying Saucers Have Landed. Revised and Enlarged Edition*
   London, UK : Neville Spearman 1970, 1972, 1976 (281 p.)
   London, UK : Futura 1977, 1978

---

1 http://ufobibliography.skepticreport.com/?p=315, retrieved 23 December 2009.
2 www.paradigmresearchgroup.org/biblio/biba.html, retrieved 23 December 2009.

Inside the Space Ships
   New York, USA : Abelard-Schuman, 1955, 1957 (256 p.)
   Toronto, Canada : Nelson, Foster and Scott Ltd, 1955 (256 p.)
   London, UK : Arco Publishers / Neville Spearman, 1956, 1957, 1958, 1966, 1971. (236 p.)
   Welwyn Garden City, Hertfordshire, UK : The Alcuin Press, 1957
   New York City, New York, USA : Fieldcrest, 1966
Re-published as: *Inside the Flying Saucers*
   New York, USA : Warner Paperback Library, 1967, 1969, 1973, 1974 (192 p.)
   Tokyo, Japan : Asahi Press, 1980 [2-volume English-language textbook with Japanese annotations]
Re-published as: *Inside the Spaceships: Ufo Experiences of George Adamski 1952-1955*
   Vista, California, USA : George Adamski Foundation International, 1980. (296 p.) [Includes Adamski's part from *Flying Saucers Have Landed.*]

Pioneers of Space : A Trip to the Moon, Mars and Venus
   Los Angeles, California, USA : Leonard Freeman Co., 1949. (260 p.)
Republished as: *The Lost Book of George Adamski – Pioneers of Space*
   New Brunswick, New Jersey, USA : Global Communications, 2008 (308 p.) [Includes a reprint of *Wisdom of the Masters of the Far East.*]
Republished as: *Pioneers of Space*
   South Boston, Virginia, USA : Black Cat Press, 2010 (207 p.)

Wisdom of the Masters of the Far East : Questions and Answers by the Royal Order of Tibet : Vol. 1
   Laguna Beach, California, USA : Royal Order of Tibet, 1936. (67 p.)
   Mokelumne Hill, California, USA : Health Research, 1974. (67 p.)
   Hastings, Sussex, UK : Society of Metaphysicians, 1986. (67 p.)
   Vista, California, USA : Science of Life, 1990.
   Pomeroy, Washington, USA : Health Research, 2000. (66 p.)
Also reprinted in *The Lost Book of George Adamski – Pioneers of Space*, New Brunswick, NJ, USA : Global Communications, 2008.

Courses

Science of Life Study Course
   [Valley Center, California, USA : G. Adamski], 1964. (12 lessons)

APPENDIX

Telepathy : The Cosmic or Universal Language
San Diego, California, USA : G. Adamski, 1958. (Parts I-III; 31, 32, 42 p.)
Vista, California, USA : Ufo Education Center/GAF, [197-?].

Bulletins and reports

Challenge to Spiritual Leaders, A
Valley Center, California, USA : G. Adamski, 1965 (3 p.) [Reprinted from C.A. Honey (ed.), *Cosmic Science* newsletter, Vol.1, No.1. January 1962.]

Cosmic Consciousness
[No details. Mentioned in Winfield Brownell, *UFOs, Keys to Earth's Destiny*, Lytle Creek, California, USA : Legion of Light Publications, 1980, p.24.]

Cosmic Science for the Promotion of Cosmic Principles and Truth : Questions and Answers
Valley Center, California, USA : Cosmic Science, 1957-58. (Parts 1-5; 16, 28, 32, 32, 36 p.)

Gravity and the Natural Forces of the Universe
[Transcript of an informal talk given in Vista, California, USA, early 1960s.] (3 p.)

In My Father's House Are Many Mansions
Detroit, Michigan, USA : Interplanetary Relations, 1955. (14 p.)
[Transcript of a press conference which Adamski held for a group of priests in September 1955, plus subsequent questions and answers.]
Re-published as: *Many Mansions*
Willowdale, Ontario, Canada : SS&S Publications, 1974, 1983 (20 p.)

Latest Fascinating Experiences
[No details. Listed in R. Michael Rasmussen, *UFO Bibliography: an annotated listing of books about flying saucers*. La Mesa, California, USA, 1975.]

Law of Levitation, The
[No details. Mentioned in Winfield Brownell, *UFOs, Keys to Earth's Destiny*, Lytle Creek, California, USA : Legion of Light Publications, 1980, p.24]

Petals of Life : Poems
   Laguna Beach, California, USA : Royal Order of Tibet, 1937. (16 p.)

Possibility of Life on Other Planets, The
   [No place], 1946. (32 p.)

Press Conference with Detroit Ministers
   Detroit, Michigan, USA : The Interplanetary Foundation, 1955. (10 p.)

Private Group Lecture for Advanced Thinkers
   Detroit, Michigan, USA : Civilian Flying Saucer Researchers, 1955. (17 p.)
   [Transcript of the CFSR's meeting with Adamski, 4 May 1955.]

Religion and Saucers
   Detroit, Michigan, USA : Interplanetary Relations, 1955. (22 p.)
   [Transcript of a lecture held in Detroit, 19 September 1955.]

Satan, Man of the Hour
   [No place; no page count], 1937.
   Reprinted (revised) in *Flying Saucers Farewell*, 1961.

Special Report : My Trip to the Twelve Counsellors' Meeting That Took Place on Saturn, March 27-30, 1962
   Vista, California, USA : Science of Life, 1962. (2 parts, 5p. + 4 p.)
   Jane Lew, West Virginia : New Age Books, 1983. (11 p.)

World of Tomorrow, The
   Detroit, Michigan, USA : Interplanetary Relations, 1956. (19 p.)
   [Transcript of a lecture held in Detroit, 20 September 1955.]

Articles/Letters

- 1937. 'The Kingdom of Heaven on Earth'. [No details. Available from GAF website.]
- 1950. 'Flying Saucers As Astronomers See Them' [with Maurice Weekly]. *FATE* magazine 3(6) : pp.56-59.
- 1951. 'I Photographed Space Ships'. *FATE* magazine 4(5): pp.64-74.
- 1955. 'Time Will Tell', *Saucerian Bulletin* No.6: p.33.

1956. 'Inside a Flying Saucer'. *Real Adventure*, July 1956: pp.40-43, pp.84-97.
1957. 'Letter about GAP'. Reprinted in Daniel Ross (ed.), *UFOs and Space Science*, No.1, December 1989, p.20.
'Flying Saucers versus the Supernatural'. *Flying Saucer Review* 3(5), p.??.
1958. 'Adamski Answers Washington Denial Regarding R. E. Straith'. *Flying Saucer Review* 4(4), pp.8-9.
1959. '*Who* is Trying to Stop the Truth Coming Out?'. *Flying Saucer Review* 5(1), pp.18-19.
1962. 'World Disturbances'. *Cosmic Science* newsletter Vol.1, No.1, January 1962, p.4.
'Positive & Negative Thinking Vs Motive'. *Cosmic Science* newsletter Vol.1, No.2, February 1962, p.4.
'George Adamski Editorial', *Cosmic Science* newsletter Vol.1, No.3, March 1962.
'Editorial by George Adamski', *Cosmic Science* newsletter Vol.1, No.4, April 1962.
'Many Are Called But Few Are Chosen', *Cosmic Science* newsletter Vol.1, No.9, September 1962, pp.1-2.
'A Challenge to Spiritual Leaders', *Cosmic Science* newsletter Vol.1, No.11, November 1962, pp.1-2.
'George Adamski's Spiritual Crusade For Survival – Results of Nuclear Testing', *Cosmic Science* newsletter Vol.1, No.12, December 1962, pp.2-3.
1964. 'Authority versus Common Sense'. *Probe* 1964. (Reprinted in Daniel Ross (ed.), *UFOs and Space Science*, No.1, December 1989., p.18-19. This issue also carried the transcript of an undated informal discussion by Adamski, which the editor titled 'Nature is the True Teacher', on p.16-17.)
'The Space People'. [Unpublished; Valley Center, California, USA]. (7 p.) Published for the first time in Part Two of the current volume.

Compilations

Adamski Documents : Part One, The [Edited by Gray Barker]
Clarksburg, West Virginia, USA : Saucerian Publications, 1980. (108 p.)
[Reprints and extracts from the author's correspondence, plus miscellaneous articles. A further compilation of correspondence to

and from George Adamski can be found as Appendix IV in Lou Zinsstag , *George Adamski – Their Man on Earth* (1990).]
Re-published as: *Adamski Papers, The*
Jane Lew, West Virginia, USA : New Age Books, 1983. (100 p.)

Answers to Questions Most Frequently Asked About Our Space Visitors And Other Planets.
Palomar Gardens, California, USA : G. Adamski, 1965. (30 p.)
[Selected questions and answers (revised) from *Cosmic Science* bulletin Series No.1, Parts 1-5 (1957-58).]

Book of Adamski [Edited by Gray Barker]
Clarksburg, West Virginia, USA : Saucerian Publications, n.d. [c1966]. (78 p.)
[Contains the following texts by George Adamski:
- 'My Fight With the Silence Group' (pp.33-37)
- 'Questions and Answers – Most frequent questions answered by George Adamski' (selection from *Cosmic Science* bulletin Series No.1, Parts 1-5, 1957-58) (pp.39-47)
- 'Space Age Philosophy' – Compilation of four undated articles: 'Positive and Negative Thinking'* ; 'Many Are Called But Few Are Chosen'*; 'How to Know A Spaceman If You See One' [1962]; and 'Annihilation' (pp.49-55)] *Reprinted articles from C.A. Honey (ed.), *Cosmic Science* newsletter Vol.1, Nos.2 and 9.]
Later reproductions:
Desert Hot Springs, California, USA : Lizardhaven Press [c1995].
Indiana, USA : Saucer's Apprentice [c2008]

Cosmic Bulletin
Valley Center, California, USA : The Adamski Foundation, 1965.
[Series of documents sent by Adamski to his followers from December 1963, until his passing in 1965.]

Notes from Adamski Lectures (1963-1964)
Valley Center, California, USA : Science of Life [196-?]. (15 p.)

Other sources

'Long-Range Telescope Added to Laguna Project', *Los Angeles Times*, 30 April 1938.

'Tibetan Monastery, First in America, to Shelter Cult Disciples in Laguna Beach', *Los Angeles Times*, 8 April 1934. (Reprinted in Hukuda Takatoshi (ed.), *Scout Ship* (newsletter of GAP-Japan Sapporo Chapter) No.4, December 1994, p.12.)

Aartsen, Gerard. 'George Adamski – A Herald for the Space Brothers', *Share International* Vol. 27, No.8, October 2008, pp.8-10.

Aartsen, Gerard. Book review *The Amazing Mr Lutterworth*, *Share International* Vol. 27, No.8, October 2008, p.11.

Aartsen, Gerard. Book review *Angels in Starships:* 'A new Moses will lead you', *Share International* Vol. 28, No.8, October 2009, pp.6-7, 18.

Bailey, Alice A. *Between War and Peace* (New York, USA : Lucis Publishing Company, 1942).

Bailey, Alice A. *From Bethlehem to Calgary* (London, UK : Lucis Press, 3rd printing, 1968).

Bailey, Alice A. *Initiation, Human and Solar* (London, UK : Lucis Press, 9th printing, 1970).

Bailey, Alice A. *A Treatise on Cosmic Fire* (London, UK : Lucis Press, 10th printing, 1973).

Bailey, Alice A. *A Treatise on The Seven Rays, Vol.I: Esoteric Psychology* (London, UK : Lucis Press, 10th printing, 1979).

Barker (ed.), Gray. *Book of Adamski* (Clarksburg, West Virginia, USA : Saucerian Publications, n.d. [c1966]).

Buckle, Eileen. *The Scoriton Mystery – Did Adamski Return?* (London, UK : Neville Spearman, 1967).

Brunt, Tony. 'George Adamski and the Toughest Job in the World' (*Secret History* Part 3, UFOCUS NZ, May 2009, http://www.ufocusnz.org.nz/secret_history_3.html, retrieved 19 December 2009).

Chapman, Robert. *UFO – Flying Saucers over Britain?* (Frogmore, St Albans, Herts, UK : Mayflower Books Ltd, 1974 reprint).

Cramp, Leonard. *Space, Gravity & The Flying Saucer* (London, UK : T. Werner Laurie, 1954).

Cranston, Sylvia. *HPB – The Extraordinary Life & Influence of Helena Blavatsky, Founder of the Modern Theosophical Movement* (USA : Tarcher/Putnam, 1993).

Creme, Benjamin. *The Art of Cooperation* (Los Angeles, USA : Share International, 2002).

Creme, Benjamin. *The Gathering of the Forces of Light – UFOs and Their Spiritual Mission* (Los Angeles, USA : Share International, 2010).

Creme, Benjamin. *The Great Approach – New Light and Life for Humanity* (Los Angeles, USA : Share International, 2001).

Creme, Benjamin. *The Reappearance of the Christ and the Masters of Wisdom* (London, UK : Tara Press, 1979).

Creme (ed.), Benjamin. *Messages from Maitreya the Christ* (London, UK : Tara Press, 1992).

Dibitonto, Giorgio. *Angels in Starships* (Phoenix, Arizona, USA : UFO Photo Archives, 1990).

Dohan, Henry. *The Pawn of His Creator – Early Contactees of Interplanetary Visitations* (Las Vegas, Nevada, USA : David R. Kammerer, 2008).

Gulyas, A.J. 'Meaningful Contact: George Adamski and the Contactees as Social Reformers'. *UFO Review* No.13, November/December 2005, pp.112-122.

Hesemann (dir.), Michael. *UFOs: The Contacts – The Pioneers of Space* (Dusseldorf, Germany : 2000 Film Productions, 1996). Re-released on DVD as *UFO Secret: Alien Contacts – The Best Evidence* (Venice, California, USA : UFO TV, 2006).

Kubota (ed.), Hachiro. *UFO Contactee*, GAP-Japan Newsletter, International Edition No.10, February 1995, pp.1-10, 12.

Leslie, Desmond. *The Amazing Mr Lutterworth*, (London, UK : Allan Wingate, 1958).

Master, Benjamin Creme's. 'The end of darkness'. *Share International*, Vol.24, No.6, July/August 2005, p.3.

Ross (ed.), Daniel. *UFOs and Space Science*, No.1, December 1989.

Zinsstag Lou & Good, Timothy. *George Adamski – The Untold Story* (Beckenham, Kent, England : CETI Publications, 1983).

Zinsstag, Lou. *George Adamski – Their Man on Earth* (Phoenix, Arizona, USA : UFO Factbook Series, 1990).

INDEX

A

Adamski, George
  a Space Brother 32, 40
  ability to explain complex principles 80
  about his own progress 94
  assault on character 64, 70
  aware of Venusian origins 56
  biographical note 19
  childhood 20
  Cosmic Philosophy 99, 101
  Cosmic Science bulletin 45, 61, 76, 77, 121
  could not tell everything he knew 14
  Flying Saucers Farewell 53, 77
  Flying Saucers Have Landed 24, 37, 43, 53, 59, 60, 121
  Foundation (G.A.F.) xi, 100
  had earlier contact with space people 56
  initiate of the Wisdom teaching 24, 27
  Inside the Space Ships 32, 39, 43, 45, 49, 52, 53, 57, 59, 74, 78, 79, 88, 100, 118
  knew about etheric levels of matter 7
  lectures around the globe 59
  obituary 12, 28
  on the Second Coming 89
  photographs of UFOs 9, 25
  Pioneers of Space – A Trip to the Moon, Mars and Venus 57
  Possibility of Life on Other Planets, The 57
  reincarnated from another planet 40, 56
  return after death 28
  Science of Life study course 67, 86
  second-degree initiate 27
  significance of his mission xi, 3, 16, 33
  simplicity of approach 61
  substance of his work 15-16
  teaching on Universal Law 71
  Telepathy, the Cosmic or Universal Language 83, 96, 115
  trained in Tibet 22, 56, 69
  trip to Saturn 8, 11
  Wisdom of the Masters of the Far East 22, 69
Ageless Wisdom teaching 6, 8, 16, 23, 26, 74, 100
Amazing Mr Lutterworth, The 38-40, 41
  correspondences with Benjamin Creme's information 41
Angels 32, 118
Angels in Starships 31, 33, 57, 118
Aquarius, Age of xi, 42, 89
Arnold, Kenneth 5
Atlantis 23
Attraction, law of 72,
Awareness, self-awakened 82

B

Bailey, Alice A. 6, 23, 35, 67

Behind the Flying Saucers 53
Blavatsky, H.P. 6, 13, 23, 70, 100
Brotherhood
  cosmic message of 84
  essential 70
  in practice 86
  indisputable fact of 71
  interplanetary xi
  law of 71, 74, 78
  of Man 92
  Universal Plan of 48
Bryant, Ernest Arthur 28, 29, 31
Buckle, Eileen 28, 31, 35
  Scoriton Mystery, The 28, 30, 32
Buddha, Maitreya 89

C

Campaign for Nuclear Disarmament (CND) 61
Cause and effect, law of 72, 74
Chapman, Robert 24
Christ 89
Cold War 4, 47
Competition
  initiative flourishes without 90
  present systems based on 90
Consciousness
  Cosmic 102
  expansion of 13, 26
  fourth dimension 86
  higher state 70
  is one 80
  is the soul 87
  life force of all forms 72
  moulds the visible from the invisible 74
Copernicus 13

Cosmic Law 5
Cosmic Philosophy 99, 101
Cosmic philosophy 39
Cosmic Science bulletin 45, 61, 76, 77, 121
Creation
  oneness with all 85
  is universal 55
Creme, Benjamin 6, 8, 14, 23, 27, 33, 41, 43, 46, 50, 63, 89
  Gathering of the Forces of Light, The 50
  work for Space Brothers 14
  worked briefly with Adamski 8
Crises, planetary 89
Crop circles 50, 56

D

Day of Declaration 42
Destiny, each must fulfil his own 94
Dibitonto, Giorgio 31, 32, 46, 48, 57, 88
  Angels in Starships 31, 57, 118
Divisions
  only created by man 86
  social 5
Djwhal Khul (DK), Master 26, 27, 63
Dohan, Henry 20, 22
  Pawn of His Creator, The 20

E

Earth
  atmospheric conditions 49
  danger threatening 48
  is kindergarten 93
  lessons of 95
  not unique 76

nothing wrong with 93
Education
  on higher planets 77-78, 93
  through space travel 91
Effectiveness
  as measured by Space Brothers 57, 61
  hindered by organizing efforts 63
Esotericism 7
Etheric levels of matter
  Adamski knew about 7
  effect of nuclear power on 50
  discovered by Wilhelm Reich 6
  life on Mars and Venus on 8

F

Fear
  of UFOs created by governments 55
  precludes encounters with Space Brothers 15
  respect will diminish 64
Firkon 32, 43, 47, 78
Flying Saucer Review 28, 53, 54
Flying Saucers Farewell 53, 77
Flying Saucers Have Landed 24, 37, 43, 53, 59, 60, 121
  Revised and enlarged edition 11
Force 74
Form 74
Free power 50, 54
Freedom 4

G

Galilei, Galileo 13
GAP-Japan 61, 64
Gathering of the Forces of Light, The 50

George Adamski – The Untold Story 12, 40
George Adamski Foundation xi, 100
Get Acquainted Program 59, 60, 64, 100
  early speculations about 58
  network of correspondents 62
  remarkably viable 63
  suggested by Space Brothers 59
Girvan, Waveney 17, 25
God, is everything in the universe 71
Good, Timothy 17
Governments, reluctance to disclose information 52
Great Society legislation 88
Greed
  has led to war with Nature 87
  present systems based on 90

H

Hubble space telescope 100
Humanity
  awakening of 46
  capability of understanding the teachings 69
  divided by criticism and prejudice 84
  has transgressed universal law 71
  pioneers of 12-13, 65
  response to new cosmic energies 89
  sense of separation 70

I

Ideologies, conflicting 4
Ilmuth 32, 43
Imam Mahdi 89

Impatience, major cause of imbalance 85
Initiation 26
Inside the Space Ships 32, 39, 45, 49, 52, 53, 57, 59, 74, 78, 79, 88, 100, 118
International Geophysical Year (IGY; 1957-58) 125

J

Jesus, Master 5, 72, 77, 78, 89
Justice 4

K

Kalki Avatar 89
Kalna 32, 43, 46
Kirlian photography 7
Knowledge, must be combined with action 128
Kubota, Hachiro 61

L

Laguna Beach 20, 56, 75
Law
  Cosmic 5
  definition 71
  of Attraction 72
  of Brotherhood 71, 74, 78
  of Cause and effect 72, 74
  of Life 71
  of Love 72
  of Patience 85
  Primary 103
  Universal 39, 56
Laws of Life 69, 74
  apply on every planet 77
  put into practice 78
  taught to people of all ages 78
Leslie, Desmond 8, 9, 14, 19, 27, 28, 29, 31, 37, 40, 42
  Amazing Mr Lutterworth, The 38-40, 41
  defence of Adamski 11, 12
  Flying Saucers Have Landed Revised and enlarged edition 11
Libraries of Recorded History 115
Life
  dense-physical x, 8, 48
  in natural state 84
  interconnectedness of 32, 86
  is One 86, 128
  oneness of 83
  purpose of 76-77, 85, 92
Los Angeles Times
  report, 30 April 1938 56, 75
  report, 8 April 1934 23
Love
  commandment of 78
  law of 72

M

Maitreya 42, 46, 89, 128
Man
  each must fulfil his own destiny 94, 113
  imposes divisions himself 86
  inherently a traveller 91
  is conglomerate of his senses 86
  is one with all creation 86
  judges another 79
  must be master of his thoughts 77, 86, 92
  must see himself as one 88
  not alone in the Universe ix
  purpose for being 76-77, 85, 92
  radiating center of influence 61, 92

separatist tendency 78
sole distorter of the Law 79
thinks form is everything 76
Mansour, Joseph 11
Marley, J. Peverell 9
Mars x, 8, 43, 51
Master
  Benjamin Creme's 27, 48, 63
  Djwhal Khul (DK)
    26, 27, 63
  Jesus 5, 72, 77, 78, 89
  Venusian 48, 49, 57,
    76, 83, 85, 93, 94, 100
Masters of Wisdom xi, 13, 22,
  23, 26, 41, 46, 56, 69,
  70, 71, 78
  use the law of Love 72
Materialism 90
Matter, difference between
  dense-physical and
  etheric 6-7, 50
Media, not interested in facts 51
Military, behind cover-ups 52
Mind
  man must master his 77, 92
  is separator 82
Money 88
  divides humanity 91
Mothership 44-45, 57

N

Nature
  greed has led to war with 87
  mother of Supreme
    Intelligence 111
New Age 89
  teachings for 70
Nuclear power
  atom bomb 4, 48
  causes most damage on
    etheric levels 50

effect on atmosphere 49
radiation depletes immune
  system 50
tests 49

O

Oneness
  of humanity 88-89
  of Life 72, 83, 86
  with creation 85
Orthon 31, 43, 51, 56, 88

P

Palomar 21, 40, 73
Patience
  law of 85
  necessary for new kind of life
    64
  weapon of Space Brothers 57
Pawn of His Creator, The 20
Peace, foundations of living
  in 79
Philosophy, true
  is science of living 76
*Pioneers of Space – A Trip to the
  Moon, Mars and Venus* 57
Planets, higher
  education begins at birth on
    77-78
  Laws of Life taught on 78
  no commercialism on 91
*Possibility of Life on Other Planets,
  The* 57
Poverty
  evil of, in the midst of plenty
    88
  leads to imbalance 88
Power
  free 50, 54
  Technology of Light 42
  UFO propulsion 51

Prophecy, definite, not possible 47
Purpose for being 76-77, 85, 92

R

Ramu (Raphael) 32, 43, 49, 57, 88
Reich, Wilhelm 6
Reincarnation 26, 28, 33, 39, 40, 74, 112
Ross, Daniel 67, 96
Roswell crash 51
Royal Order of Tibet 20, 56

S

Saturn 43, 112
  Adamski's trip to 8, 11
Science
  limitations of present 5
  of life, taught on neighbouring planets 77
  of living 76
Science of Life study course 67, 86
Scoriton Mystery, The 28, 30, 32
Scout ship 10, 43
Scully, Frank 53
  Behind the Flying Saucers 53
Second Coming 46, 89
Self-knowledge 77, 83
Self, real
  one with Cosmos 83
Senses
  man must learn to control 85
  we judge through our 84
Service 113
  as means to self-knowledge 24
Sherwood, William 14
Silence Group 54

Skeptics 11, 15, 57, 70
Social
  change 70
  divisions 5
  freedom 4
  justice 4
Society of Psychical Research 13
Space Brothers 5, 41, 42, 43
  also travel pathway of life 91
  are here to protect and help us 46
  as angels 32, 118
  clean up nuclear radiation 50
  come in friendship 84
  coming to aid humanity in transition 70
  do not judge or condemn 79, 84
  do not prophesy 63
  emphasize need to live the teachings 63
  have control over their minds 77, 86
  have passed through the same experiences 95
  leaving evidence 50, 51, 56
  live in compassionate humility 87
  live the Universal Laws 78
  living among us 59, 78, 83, 91, 125
  made contact with leaders of every nation 46
  not here to satisfy our curiosity 64
  possible broadcast from 42
  'Roswell' was deliberate sacrifice on the part of 51
  spiritual life of 117
  spiritual mission of 50

INDEX

study life 86
suggested Get Acquainted
  Program 59
teachings of 16, 74
type of help 47
visits in olden times 48
Space craft 10, 44-45
  as modern-day 'stars of
    Bethlehem' 41-42
  keeping a constant vigil 125
  propulsion 51
'Star' of Bethlehem 41-42
Steckling, Fred 34
Stevens, Wendelle C. 33

T

Technology of Light 42
  crop circles 50, 56
  free power 42, 50, 54
*Telepathy, the Cosmic or Universal
  Language* 83, 96, 115
Temple of Scientific Philosophy
  56, 75
Thoughts
  man must learn to control
    his 77, 86, 92
  Space Brothers are masters of
    their 77, 86, 113
Tibet 22, 23, 56, 69
Time magazine xi
Travel
  practical education 91
  time for 90

U

UFOs
  as modern-day 'stars of
    Bethlehem' 41-42
  create spiritual platform 47
  fear of, created by
    governments 55
  military behind cover-ups 52
'Uncle Sid' 20, 22, 23, 56
United Nations Organization 39
Unity, keynote of the New
  Age 42, 89
Universal Law 39, 56
  brotherhood 71, 74
  handed down through the
    ages 76, 78
  implementing, in our own life
    91-92
  instruction given in 78
  must be learned and applied
    79
  principles of 79-80
  understanding of, uplifts and
    restricts 94
Universe 72, 85

V

Venus x, 8, 43, 111-126
Venusian Master 48, 49, 57,
  76, 83, 85, 93, 94, 100

W

*Wisdom of the Masters of the Far
  East* 22, 69
World Teacher xi, 41, 42, 46
  reappearance of 47, 89

Y

'Yamski' 29

Z

Zinsstag, Lou 12, 13, 20, 22,
  25, 40, 52, 53, 56, 61
  *George Adamski – The Untold
    Story* 12, 40
Zuhl 32, 43
Zurich incident 53

145

By the same author:

Our Elder Brothers Return –
A History in Books (1875 – Present)
published online at www.biblioteca-ga.info

Here to Help: UFOs and the Space Brothers

The author may be contacted at
info@bgapublications.nl